THE **LONDON CAFÉ** BOOK

the London café book

AUTHOR
SIMON GARNER

PHOTOGRAPHER
GILES STOKOE

vega

AN IMPRINT OF
SALAMANDER BOOKS LIMITED

a **vega** book

An imprint of Salamander Books Ltd
8 Blenheim Court, Brewery Road
London N7 9NT
United Kingdom

ISBN 1 84065 056 7

Commissioning Editor
Helen Stone
Designer
Graham Mitchener
Reproduction
CS Graphics Pte Ltd, Singapore

9 8 7 6 5 4 3 2 1

Printed and bound in Singapore

Acknowledgments
The author would like to thank: Britta Martins for suggesting that
I could do this, Helen, Giles and Graham for being so easy to
work with and all of the café owners and staff for their
helpfulness and tolerance.

The photographer would like to thank: Helen for conceiving the
book and making it all happen, my wife Jo for putting up with
me during its production, and Simon for his patience, helping me
with all my gear and for saying I was easy to work with. I would
also like to thank all the café owners for so freely giving up so
much time and energy.

The publishers would like to thank all the café owners, chefs and
staff, both from those venues featured in this book and from
those which took the time to help with initial research. Thanks go
to all the people who kindly gave their permission for us to
reproduce their words and images.

Contents

Café /ˈkæfeɪ,
ˈkæfɪ/n.
(also **cafe** /
also joc. kæf,
keɪf/) ɪ. a small
coffee-house
or teashop;
a simple
restaurant.

The Concise Oxford Dictionary of Current English, eighth edition, 1990

London

isn't famous for its cafés; it never has been. It isn't Paris or Vienna or Berlin; it is London, an altogether more mixed and varied place and consequently, in my opinion at least, the most interesting city in Europe. The things that make London so exciting are the very same things that can make it frustrating to the casual visitor and resident alike: the fact that it is big, sprawling and inaccessible; the fact that its best features are often distant and hard to find; the fact that it is rarely obvious. Outside of the usual tourist traps, where you are supposed to go, London is a large, lazy, complacent sort of place which tends to keep its treasures to itself, and that is why it is also full of surprises. Around every corner there is a discovery; a concealed park, a picturesque back street, a cemetery, a bar, a restaurant and, of course, often when you least expect it, a

café

. The aim of this book is to reveal a few of those secrets. It is an attempt to communicate, in pictures and in words, some sense of the variety of London café life and cuisine. It is not a guide book, a critique nor a comprehensive survey, but a

photographic

portrait of a small selection of disparate and unusual cafés, all of which, we hope, have something special to offer; whether it is the decor, the location, the owner, the clientele or the food itself. Each of them should be one of those little discoveries that makes London such a perennially fascinating place. Making the decisions as to which venues to include was not easy. We have tried to present a good

cross-section

and cover most areas of London, although obviously there is a concentration in Soho. Our only criterion was that each place should be a café; but, as we found during the course of researching the book, a café is not always an easy thing to define. In fact, as with a lot of things, it is easier to say what it isn't. It isn't a pub, a bar, a restaurant, a brasserie or a bistro. We came up with a number of factors to guide us.

A café should be a place where conversation is fuelled by caffeine and not by alcohol.

It should be a place where you do not have to eat but where you can if you want to and, if you do, you should be able to get a reasonably-priced, one-stop meal. It should be a place where you can go on your **own** and not feel awkward. It should be a place where it is perfectly acceptable to linger over a paperback or a newspaper. All these things, we decided, are essential to the nature of a café; but they are not decisive. There is one other factor that sets cafés apart from bistros, bars and brasseries and that factor is:

cake.

If you can order coffee and cake, a place is a café. Cake is the factor that gets rid of what we came to call the 'tea-room-dilemma'. Tea rooms, we decided, are cafés and therefore should be included in this book; they are cafés not just because the dictionary definition says so but because they pass the cake test. In fact, the only place included in this book that fails on the cake criterion is M. Manze, but a pie and mash shop is so photogenic and so essentially London that we decided to bend the rules a little to include it. Cake, of course, does not explain everything. It doesn't explain why, if you start taking photographs in a café, there is invariably at least one other

photographer among the customers. It doesn't explain why nearly a third of London's most attractive looking cafés turn out to be hairdresser's or the fact that such a high percentage of café owners turn out to be former

interior designers.

But it does provide a useful touchstone to let you know whether the place you are sitting in can really count as a café. And hopefully this book succeeds in communicating a sense of the great variety of London café life – it really isn't homogeneous enough to call it

café society.

If it is half as much fun to read as it was to write it will have achieved its goal; but if you decide to visit any of the places included on the following pages, do remember that caffeine can seriously damage your health.

6 We all drink too much coffee on the whole; it is abused; it is not meant to be gulped down indiscriminately. I would rather drink one good cup of coffee a day and set aside the time to enjoy it. Anita Le Roy, Proprietor 9

Monmouth Coffee Company

27 Monmouth Street
London WC2H 9DD

The starting point of any good café is the coffee itself; and the starting point of good coffee is the beans. At Monmouth Coffee Company, Anita Le Roy and her staff deal directly with the raw ingredient. Green beans arrive here in sacks from all over the world, are loaded into silos and carefully roasted in the cellar before being packaged for sale. Customers can sample the wide range of beans, roasts and blends in the sampling room at the rear of the shop before making a purchase; or they can just stand outside and savour the magnificent smell.

11

"There is no guaranteed formula; roasting coffee is very intuitive. Every coffee is different and every shipment is different. After each roast we taste and assess it."
Anita Le Roy

The Perfect Cup of Coffee

You can make a delicious cup of coffee using a filter; you don't need a machine, just a cup or warmed jug, a filter cone and paper, boiling water and of course some really good, freshly-roasted coffee.

Put a generous amount of ground coffee in the filter paper; don't be mean with it; if it is too strong you can dilute it with a little hot water but if it is too weak you are stuck with it. Bring a kettle of freshly drawn water to the boil and let it cool a little (count to 10). Now the most important part: trickle a little hot water over the grounds to moisten them and leave for a few seconds; this 'primes' or softens the coffee so that when you pour on the rest of the water you will draw the maximum flavour from the grounds. Now you can gradually pour on the rest of the water and your coffee is ready to serve.

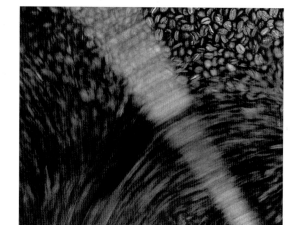

13

When coffee is this good,
who needs espresso?

Any café which names itself after its pastry chef clearly takes its
cakes very seriously. Ugo Amato was the head pastry chef
at Patisserie Valerie for fifteen years before setting up Amato with Renzo
Rapacioli. Amato is managed by Renzo's son, Daniel.

Amato

14 Old Compton Street
London W1V 5PE

The Soho café is an institution in itself; a place for the motley life of London's most lively area to avoid the crush and bustle of the streets and mull over paperbacks and newspapers in a relaxed atmosphere whilst sipping an espresso. Amato fits the bill so perfectly that it is hard to believe it has only been here two years. It is the Soho café par excellence: classic decor, friendly staff, a lively atmosphere and, most importantly, pastries and cakes to die for.

15

Amato recently
won the 1997
Evening Standard
award for
the best cup
of coffee in
London.

For Daniel, the
making of coffee
is a precise
science.
Everything is
taken into
account: the blend
of the beans;
the temperature
and
pressure
of the water; even
the shape and
warmth
of the cups.

Claudia Manzoni studied catering in Italy. She has been working at Amato since she took refuge in the café during a bomb scare and Daniel offered her a job.

" We argue a lot . . . I like it.
Claudia Manzoni,
Manager's Assistant

17

The neat, waistcoated staff are probably the friendliest in London.

"They're really happy, smiley people for some unknown reason . . . actually we inject them with caffeine in the mornings."
Daniel Rapacioli,
Café Manager

" Smoking is part of café life . . . as the walls get darker, we put in brighter bulbs. People complain that it is too light . . . but, if they want it dark, they can always wear sunglasses.
Daniel Rapacioli

> Customers don't come first, coffee and cakes do.
> **Daniel Rapacioli**, Café Manager

18

The cakes might come first, but Amato also has a savoury menu including all-day breakfasts, sandwiches and pasta specials.

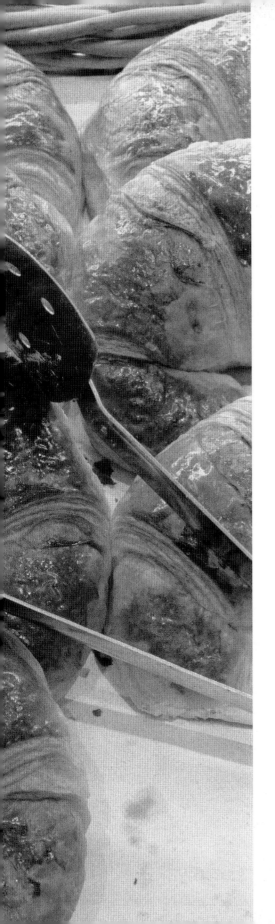

Torinese Gâteau   serves 8–12
(ingredients)

Chocolate and Hazelnut Sponge
6 egg yolks, 160g (5½oz) sugar,
5 egg whites, 100g (3½oz) self-raising
flour, 40g (1½oz) cornflour, 40g (1½oz)
ground hazelnuts, 40g (1½oz) cocoa powder

Giandua Cream
½ litre (18fl oz) milk, 75g (2¾oz) sugar,
4 egg yolks, 30g (1¼oz) plain flour,
150g (5½oz) dark chocolate, 50g (1¾oz)
hazelnut paste, ½ litre (18fl oz) whipping
cream

+

rum liqueur, plain syrup (boiled sugar and
water), ½ litre (18fl oz) whipping cream,
1 tablespoon sugar, ½kg (1lb 2oz) dark
chocolate, icing sugar, cocoa powder

20

Torinese Gâteau (how to make)

Pre-heat the oven to 180C (350F/gas mark 4). To make the sponge, whisk the egg yolks with 100g (3½oz) of the sugar until light. In a separate bowl, whisk the egg whites with 60g (2oz) of sugar until light and fluffy. Mix the two together and fold in the flour, cornflour, hazelnuts and cocoa powder to make a smooth, thick chocolate liquid. Pour the mixture into a 20cm (8in) cake tin and bake for 30 minutes.

To make the cream, heat the milk, sugar and egg yolks together in a heavy-based saucepan and stir in the flour until smooth. Bring to the boil and simmer until the mixture becomes like cream, then add the dark chocolate (broken into pieces) and the hazelnut paste. Stir until the chocolate has dissolved. Remove from the heat, cool and place in the refrigerator until chilled. Whip the cream, fold it into the chocolate cream and return to the refrigerator.

To assemble the gâteau, slice the chocolate and hazelnut sponge horizontally into three even layers and soak with a sauce of rum liqueur and plain syrup. Spread the Giandua cream evenly over the top of two of the slices of sponge and reassemble the sponge into a sandwich. Whip the remaining cream with 1 tablespoon of sugar and cover the top and sides of the sponge. Melt the chocolate in a bowl over a pan of boiling water. Pour the chocolate onto a cool surface and spread evenly with a palette knife, continuing the motion until it hardens. Scrape the chocolate off in long strips. Attach strips of chocolate to the top and sides of the cake, then sprinkle the top with icing sugar and cocoa powder.

Bar Italia occupies the ground floor of the house where **John Logie Baird** first demonstrated television in **1926**.

Bar Italia's original interior has been home to countless Soho **encounters**. It is so famous there is even a **Pulp** song named after it.

Bar Italia

22 Frith Street
London W1V 5TS

Soho would not really be Soho without Bar Italia – a 24-hour Italian coffee bar which has been dispensing caffeine fixes to the sleepless denizens of Frith Street since 1949. During the day the neat, white-shirted and black-tied staff serve a constant stream of customers, but it is at night that Bar Italia really comes alive; fashionable young clubbers, the world-weary and the plain eccentric spill out onto the streets to enjoy a final cappuccino. There is no better place to wait for your night bus.

Bar Italia
True Italian Espresso & Cappuccino

23

Bar Italia was founded by Lou Polledri and was opened by **Abbot and Costello** and **Ronnie Scott** in 1949. It has been in the family ever since and is currently run by Tony and Louigie Polledri – Lou's grandchildren.

TV is part of Bar Italia **culture**. At 7.00pm every evening, the huge screen turns over to Italian news and Bar Italia fills with **old-time Italians** catching up on current events and talking **politics**. It also covers all major footballing events.

In 1982 over 120 people crowded into Bar Italia to watch the **World Cup** final. The atmosphere was so humid that the television broke down. Everybody started screaming at me . . . I knew my **life** was on the line. At half-time I managed to borrow a set from next door . . . and Italy, of course, went on to **win** the World Cup.
Tony Polledri, Proprietor

"We do as little as possible to it . . . just **essential** repairs. We try to keep it all **original**."
Tony Polledri

The picture of **Rocky Marciano** on the wall is not just retro chic. Rocky was a friend of Lou Polledri and, when Rocky died, the picture was sent over from the **USA** by his widow.

25

The world-**famous** coffee at Bar Italia is blended on the premises to a **secret** family recipe.

"The coffee here is like velvet."
Sarah Gantz,
Customer

❛ I've been here **every day** for two years . . . it's like coming to the **office** . . . a reason to get up in the morning. ❜ Sarah Gantz

GAGGIA

Artichoke, Parma Ham and Sundried Tomato Toasted Ciabatta Sandwich

per serving

1 portion of Ciabatta bread
olive oil
fresh ground pepper
marinated artichoke hearts, sliced
2 thin slices of Parma ham
sundried tomatoes
sea salt (optional)
salad to garnish

Slice the Ciabatta down the middle and lightly toast. Drizzle olive oil over both halves of the bread and sprinkle one with fresh ground pepper. Lay the sliced artichoke hearts on one half of the bread, then cover with the slices of Parma ham. Arrange the sundried tomatoes on top of the ham and sprinkle with sea salt if desired. Replace the second half of the bread and serve with a salad garnish.

27

Every Wednesday evening English motorbike owners congregate outside Bar Italia, while on the last Thursday of every month, it is a meeting place for Harley Davidson owners.

"It's like World War III out there . . . you need earplugs." Tony Polledri

Deep Fried Mozzarella

per serving

150g (5½oz) Mozzarella
beaten egg
breadcrumbs
oil for frying

Slice the Mozzarella into 2cm (¾in) thick rounds (if the Mozzarella you have is small and round, cut it into wedges). Dip the cheese into the beaten egg. Pour the breadcrumbs onto a plate and roll the egg-coated cheese in the crumbs until it is thoroughly coated. Heat the oil in a pan until sizzling hot and deep fry the Mozzarella until the crumb coating turns a golden brown. Remove the cheese from the oil and drain on kitchen paper to remove any excess oil.

Deep fried Mozzarella is delicious served hot on a bed of freshly-cooked spinach, served with a tomato-based sauce and anchovies.

Bar Italia serves a range of ciabatta sandwiches and light meals but, for more substantial fare, go next door to Little Italy. Also run by Tony and Louigie Polledri, Bar Italia's sister restaurant is licensed till 3.00am and serves modern Italian food into the small hours.

The colourful totem pole that dominates the room from an alcove was a former theatre prop. It may look heavy but in fact it is made of polystyrene.

Blue Legume

101 Stoke Newington Church Street
London N16 OUD

A few years ago there would have been little to tempt the casual visitor to Stoke Newington. These days, however, Church Street has a village atmosphere; craft, antique, and clothes shops sit side by side with a range of popular restaurants. At the heart of Church Street, Louise Ratcliffe and her partner, Jonathan Early, have succeeded in creating one of the most inviting spaces in North London: a small but perfectly formed café sporting one of the most imaginative menus in the city.

31

Each June, Blue Legume plays a leading role in the Stoke Newington Mid-summer Festival; tables and stalls spill out onto the road and a party atmosphere takes over Church Street.

The striking **mosaic-topped** tables were made by Louise and Jonathan during the long winter **evenings** while they were waiting to arrange the lease.

"We wanted it to look like we'd been here **forever**; we even put nicotine glop on the walls." Louise Ratcliffe, Proprietor

The food served in Blue Legume is a reflection of the sort of food Louise
and Jonathan like to eat themselves.

Our **philosophy** has been to take everything that is good about
vegetarian food but to combine it with **organic meat**
and fish dishes. **Jonathan Early**, Proprietor

Blue Legume
has provided
food for Hackney
Council, Action
Time TV and
**Channel
Four**. Louise
and Jonathan are
currently
expanding their
kitchen to be
able to take on
more outside
catering
work.

Blue legume serves a wide range of drinks: from
organic wine and porter to barley cup and **soyaccinno**
– a cappuccino made with soya milk ". . . so that the vegans feel like
they can join in . . . they can't have chocolate on the top though."
Louise Ratcliffe

33

During the day the range of food is **displayed** behind a glass counter. "The idea is that people can **see** the food; we don't have a **table menu**." Louise Ratcliffe

The Blue Legume serves a selection of **salads** all year round. "In **winter** people come in saying, 'Give me some **fresh veg**.'" Louise Ratcliffe

"I come in here every Friday afternoon to **relax** after work."
Gillian Dyson,
Local Head Teacher

"The food here is **wonderful**.
Denise Robson, Local
Government officer and Labour Party
candidate for Maidenhead

Chicken and Bacon Balls on Spaghetti

serves 4

Chicken and Bacon Balls	Sauce
1 large Spanish onion, chopped	1 large Spanish onion, chopped
groundnut oil	groundnut oil
2 free-range chicken breasts, roughly chopped	425g (15oz) tin chopped plum tomatoes
8 rashers of smoked bacon, roughly chopped	1 tablespoon tomato purée
1 teaspoon crushed garlic	1 glass red wine
salt and pepper	salt and pepper
6 stems of fresh basil	
fresh breadcrumbs	

+

4 portions of spaghetti

crème fraîche, black pepper and 1 stem of fresh basil to garnish

To make the meat balls, sauté the onion in groundnut oil until translucent, cool, then add the remainder of ingredients and mince together in a food processor. Add sufficient breadcrumbs to stiffen the mixture. Leave in the refrigerator to set for approximately 1 hour. When cool, divide the mixture into 16 portions and shape each into a ball.

To make the sauce, sauté the onion, then add the tomatoes, tomato purée and red wine and bring the mixture to the boil. Lower the temperature and simmer and reduce for approximately 20 minutes. Season to taste.

Add the chicken balls to the sauce and continue to cook for a further 20 minutes. Cook the spaghetti and serve immediately topped with four meat balls per person and a generous ladle of sauce. Top with a dollop of crème fraîche, ground black pepper and fresh torn basil.

Sweet Potato, Leek, Brie and Apple Strudel

serves 4

1kg (2lb 4oz) sweet potatoes
knob of butter
salt and pepper
potato powder (to thicken)
1 large Spanish onion, chopped
3 leeks, chopped
groundnut oil
250g (9oz) Brie, roughly chopped
2 dessert apples, peeled, cored, grated and sprinkled with lemon juice
1 packet filo pastry, cut into 20 x 10cm (8 x 4in) pieces — 5 for each strudel
beaten egg for glazing
sunflower seeds

Pre-heat the oven to 190C (375F/gas mark 5). Peel and boil the sweet potatoes
then mash with butter and season to taste. Add a little potato powder to make
the mixture workable and not sticky. Sauté the onion and leeks in groundnut oil
until soft, then fold them into the potato mixture along with the roughly-chopped
Brie. Fold the apple into the mixture and allow to cool.
To make each strudel, lay a sheet of filo on an oiled baking sheet, brush with oil
and lay a second sheet of filo on top. Divide the potato mixture into four and
spoon a sausage of the mixture onto each of the four portions of filo. Cover the
filling with three sheets of filo, brushing with oil between each layer. Brush the
strudels with beaten egg and sprinkle sunflower seeds on top. Bake in the middle of
the oven for 15–20 minutes or until golden.

Blue Mountain

18 North Cross Road
London SE22 9EU

In a former dairy in a quiet side street in East Dulwich, Mel Nugent has succeeded in creating a café quite unlike any other. Strikingly imaginative interior design has been used to transform each of the small individual rooms into a visual feast. The rustic and distressed downstairs decor exudes an intimate, relaxed charm; while the bright, clean modernism of the upstairs room provides a starker environment in which to enjoy a coffee or sample the excellent and varied international cooking.

39

6 I wanted to conjure up this idea of the shops in my local area in **Jamaica**: kind of **shacky**; nice colours; almost tumble-down but laid back . . . they always used corrugated iron . . . so we came up with the idea of using the corrugated iron as a **lamp shade**. *9*
Mel Nugent, Proprietor

The extraordinary decor was created by Mel and his **decorator**, Gary Weekes. "**Gary** is great – he interprets what I want . . . he's **brilliant** . . . he really is." Mel Nugent

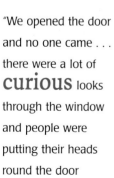

"We opened the door and no one came . . . there were a lot of **curious** looks through the window and people were putting their heads round the door and saying, **'What are you selling in here . . . antiques?'"**
Mel Nugent

Mel, a former delicatessen manager, has come a long way since his training with Trusthouse Forte. He still has fond memories of playing football in his chef's whites outside Scratchwood service station.

' It's the only place round here . . . it's the best cappuccino you can get for ten miles.
Simon Bligh, Customer '

After the heavily-distressed charm of the downstairs rooms, the stark, simple modernism of the upstairs room may come as a shock.

"We keep the food really open; our chef, Bea Mundle, changes the menu daily. We do have more of a vegetarian slant, but we recognize that there are robust meat eaters out there."
Mel Nugent

Fusilli Tutti Freschi

serves 4

700g (1lb 9oz) cooked fusilli pasta
40ml (1½fl oz) walnut oil
100g (3½oz) red and yellow peppers,
    blanched
100g (3½oz) courgettes, cut into sticks
40g (1½oz) spring onions, chopped
100g (3½oz) raw mushrooms, sliced
40g (1½oz) flaked almonds
25g (1oz) mixed robot chillies
25g (1oz) garlic purée
fresh coriander, finely chopped

Cook the pasta in boiling water until al
dente. Heat the walnut oil in a pan or wok
until the oil is very hot. Add all the
ingredients except the pasta and coriander
and fry until al dente and lightly browned.
Add the fusilli pasta and toss. Sprinkle with
coriander and serve when the pasta is heated
through.

43

Tuscan salad

serves 8 (starter portions)

1 large bag of baby spinach
2 raddichio, roughly sliced
1 red pepper, de-seeded and sliced
1 yellow pepper, de-seeded and sliced
1 green pepper, de-seeded and sliced
olive oil
225g (8oz) mushrooms, sliced thinly
100g (3½oz) sundried tomatoes
300ml (½ pint) French dressing
2 tablespoons red pesto

Pre-heat the oven to 190C (375F/gas mark 5). Wash and drain the spinach and raddichio leaves and toss together. Arrange the pepper slices on a baking sheet, drizzle with olive oil and roast until golden brown. Remove from the oven and allow the peppers to cool. Toss the cooled peppers with the salad leaves, mushrooms and sundried tomatoes. Mix the salad dressing with the red pesto and add just enough dressing to the salad to coat the leaves before serving.

44

'I like everything here except the chairs. The food is great, the cakes are great, the coffee is great . . . but the furniture is terrible.
Joel Rubin, Customer'

"We're always on the lookout for more uncomfortable chairs."
Mel Nugent

The name was a moment of inspiration...
well, actually, it was the only thing we could cook.
Sue Sutton, Proprietor

The Boiled Egg & Soldiers

63 Northcote Road
London SW11 1NP

Midway between Clapham and
Wandsworth Commons, Northcote
Road is rapidly becoming the
gastronomic centre of this bijou
area of south-west London. Among
a variety of bars and restaurants,
The Boiled Egg & Soldiers stands
out as exceptional. It is a caff with
a difference: the atmosphere is
airy and bright; the portions are
large; and the quality of the
produce excellent.

When The Boiled Egg & Soldiers opened in December 1995, owners, Sara Stickland and Sue Sutton attempted a low key opening. They seriously underestimated the popularity of their all-day breakfasts. "We ran out of everything. I had my kids washing up. It was a complete fiasco . . . oh yes, and the chef resigned on the first day, but was gallant enough not to leave until we had found a replacement."

Sara Stickland, Proprietor

SPECIALS

...AM OF CELERY.

OLD ENGLISH PORK & PORK & LEEK,

...roissant with onion, mushroom £3.25.

...d cheese. ...ee with bread & butter. £3.95

...terranean Cheesecake served £3.95 with Salad

with Poached Eggs & Black Pudding £3.75 delicious Mustard Sauce

ORANGE & BLUEBERRY £1.25

STICKY GINGER Coffee & walnut. ...ocolate Brownie ...ry flapjack £2.25

The philosophy behind the food is simple, fresh, comfort food. We don't try to be too clever; we are a café not a restaurant. We have no pretensions to being restaurateurs or chefs but, what we do, we try to do really well. Sara Stickland

Sue and Sara, both former interior designers, had no previous experience of running a café. "We're not foodies . . . we are punters." Sara Stickland

Sara and Sue will **hand-pick** an appropriate **tea pot** for their customers from the colourful selection on the shelves behind the counter.

If we get a big, burly builder, we try to give him a **pink** *one.*
Sara Stickland

During the week, The Boiled Egg & Soldiers is popular with kids, **mums** and nannies. At the weekends, the clientele changes and local residents queue at the door for a **carbohydrate fix** to cure their hangovers.

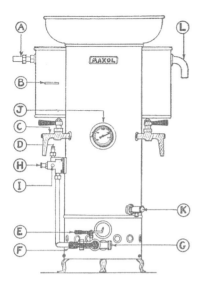

A huge Maxol 'T' water boiler dominates the room. Sara and Sue still have the original instruction manual on which a hand written note states: 'Water boiler has been installed on the day Wednesday 7/3/ 1956 6pm.'

In April 1995, when they were looking for premises for their new project, Sara and Sue stumbled upon the Olympic Restaurant. They struck up an immediate friendship with the 78-year-old owner, George Procopiou. He offered them the lease and told them, 'I'd rather take my coat and lock the door and leave it empty than let someone I don't like have it.'

The Fluffy

One of the house specialities, the Fluffy is essentially just milk, making it popular with mums and nannies. The children love it too as it tastes good and is fun to eat.

To make your own Fluffy, you will need a cappuccino maker. Gently foam a cup of semi-skimmed milk until the foam has the consistency of uncooked meringue. Spoon the foam into an espresso cup, sprinkle with drinking chocolate powder and serve.

The Boiled Egg & Soldiers may only have been here for a little under **two years**, but the premises have been a **café** for much longer. It was the Oak Tree Café for thirty-two years and then the Olympic Restaurant for forty-eight years.

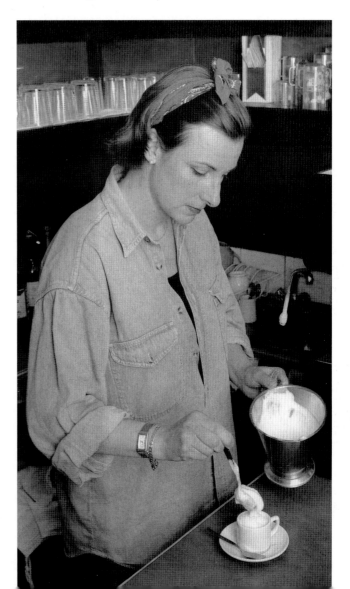

51

Muffins with Poached Egg, Black Pudding and Mustard Sauce

per serving

1 English muffin
2 large eggs
2 slices of good quality black pudding
butter
½ teaspoon English mustard
½ teaspoon French mustard
½ teaspoon coarse grain mustard
1 teaspoon balsamic vinegar
1½ tablespoons Greek yoghurt

Split the muffin and toast lightly. In the meantime, poach the eggs and grill the black pudding. Make the sauce by mixing the mustards, balsamic vinegar and yoghurt together – you can calm the sauce if it is too hot by adding more yoghurt. Lightly butter the muffin, place a slice of black pudding on each half and top with the poached eggs. Serve immediately with the mustard sauce.

"We don't skimp . . . all our eggs are large." Sue Sutton

Sue, Sara and Sara's husband,
Jonathan, met at college.

I could have **married** Sue,
but I chose **him** instead.
Sara Stickland

There are two things that people always exclaim when they come in, 'I can't believe these are all cook books' and, 'It smells so good in here.'
Rosie Kindersley, Book Shop Manager

Books for Cooks

4 Blenheim Crescent,
London W11 1NN

Since it was established in 1983 by Heidi Lascelles, Books for Cooks has become something of a legend – it is London's only book shop dedicated entirely to cookery; but it is more than just a book shop. Food here is not just something to be perused in books, it is something to be made. At the back of the book shop, in a tiny café with an even smaller kitchen, the staff of Books for Cooks put theory into practice, serving up coffee, fantastic home-baked cakes and splendid lunches.

Upstairs at Books for Cooks, there is a larger **demonstration** kitchen where Eric Treuille, Ursula Ferrigno and other **guest chefs** run regular cookery classes.

"We don't have **celebrity** chefs . . . they have too big a following and we don't have the space."
Eric Treuille, Chef

It has to be London's **smallest** café . . . I can't believe there's one smaller. If we got **bigger**, we'd become like everybody else.
Rosie Kindersley

"It is more than just a café; it is a kitchen **laboratory** where people come to test things and **experiment** and develop new **recipes**." Rosie Kindersley

We have
everything
here: *Cooking with
Cannabis,
The Roadkill
Cookbook,
The Life and
Cuisine of Elvis
Presley* and loads
and loads of
love and
sex books . . .
we even have *The
History of
Cannibalism.* Rosie
Kindersley

"This place couldn't have worked if it had appeared anywhere else . . . there's the veg market and we couldn't do without it . . . there's everything we want on the doorstep . . . it's a product of multicultural London. We're an intrinsic part of the Portabello theme park." Rosie Kindersley

All the food served
in the café is
cooked from
scratch every
day. We do
everything from
the first cup of
flour to the last bit
of washing up
. . . it's real
cooking for real
people.
Celia
Brooks-
Brown, Chef

"This is what it is
about at Books for
Cooks; you never
know who is
going to walk
through the door
. . . big chefs . . .
small chefs . . .
anyone."
Eric Treuille

Celia's Chocolate Banana Mascarpone Cheesecake *serves 8-12*

Crust
200g (7oz) plain chocolate wholewheat biscuits, crushed
60g (2oz) butter, melted

Filling
500g (1lb) cream cheese, softened
240g (8oz) caster sugar
2 free-range eggs, beaten
250g (8oz) Mascarpone
2 teaspoons vanilla extract
2 ripe (but not brown) bananas, sliced

Topping
90g (3oz) plain chocolate
60g (2oz) butter
1 banana
lemon juice
chocolate curls to decorate

"Good cooking attracts other cooks." Rosie Kindersley

Pre-heat the oven to 180C (350F/gas mark 4). To make the crust, mix the biscuit crumbs and melted butter together, press evenly into the bottom of a 24cm (9½in) springform cake tin and bake for 10 minutes. Reduce the oven temperature to 160C (325F/gas mark 3) and allow the crust to cool while you make the filling. Beat the cream cheese, then beat in the sugar, eggs, Mascarpone, vanilla and bananas. Pour into the cake tin and bake for 30-40 minutes until just set (placing a bowl of water below the cake as it cooks prevents a skin forming). Run a knife around the edge of the tin as soon as the cheesecake comes out of the oven and then leave the cake in its tin to cool before chilling in the refrigerator for at least 3 hours or overnight.

About an hour before serving, slice the bananas and soak them in lemon juice. Melt the chocolate and butter for the topping in a bowl over a saucepan of hot water. Unmould the cake and pour on the chocolate topping. Dry the banana slices on kitchen paper and arrange them on top of the cake along with chocolate curls. Chill for another 30 minutes before indulging.

Skewers of Marinated Chicken   serves 4

Skewers

4 chicken breasts, skinned and boned

12 slices of prosciutto, cut in half

1/2 french stick, cut into 2.5cm
   (1in) cubes (32 in total)

24 fresh sage leaves (or fresh rosemary)

2 garlic cloves, peeled and crushed

grated zest and juice of 1 lemon

150ml (8fl oz) olive oil

salt and pepper

8 wooden skewers, soaked in water

Salad

8 ripe plum tomatoes, halved

18 spring onions, cut into strips

6 tablespoons crème fraîche

coriander sprigs

lemon olive oil

sea salt and coarsely ground black
   pepper

Pre-heat the oven to 180C (350F/gas mark 4). Cut each chicken breast into 6 evenly-sized pieces and wrap each in a slice of prosciutto – you will need 3 pieces of chicken, 4 cubes of bread and 3 herb sprigs per skewer. Thread a bread cube onto a skewer, followed by a herb sprig and then a chicken piece and continue in this way until all the skewers are threaded. Mix together the garlic, lemon zest and juice, olive oil and seasoning and pour over the skewers to marinate. Cover and chill for a few hours, turning the skewers in the marinade from time to time. Place the tomato halves cut-side down in a roasting dish, sprinkle with oil and salt and roast for 20 minutes until soft. Grill or dry-fry the spring onions until wilted and slightly charred. Grill both sides of the skewers until the chicken is cooked through and the bread is crispy.

To serve, place 4 roasted tomato halves cut-side down to one side of each plate. Spoon a dollop of crème fraîche in the middle of the tomatoes and scatter with spring onions and coriander sprigs. Sprinkle with olive oil and salt and pepper. Arrange the chicken skewers on the other side of the plate and serve at once.

6 When the food runs out, it runs out . . . but we do get people begging. Rosie Kindersley 9

Candid
Café

3 Torrens Street
London EC1V 1NQ

Occupying a long window-lined room on the second floor of an old British Rail parcels office behind Angel Islington station, Candid Café is one of the best kept secrets in London. Battered armchairs, sofas, a huge long table and various artworks create a startlingly bohemian atmosphere. But behind the scenes, Candid Café is far more than it appears to be; it is, in fact, part of the Candid Arts Trust – an organization set up in 1989 by Duncan Barlow and Maria Avino to promote a multi-media approach to the arts. Elsewhere in the rambling building, there are artists' studios, a banqueting hall and two large loft-style gallery spaces.

63

Visit the Candid Arts Trust on the web at **http://www.candidarts.com**

"Educating the public is a big part of what we do and the café is quite instrumental in that . . . people come in just wanting a cup of coffee and they get absorbed into what is happening . . . but not in a pretentious way." Duncan Barlow, Arts Trust Founder

Duncan was the first person to bring mixed media under one roof . . . everyone does it now but, at the time, it was totally unacceptable to put jewellers with fine art . . . but Duncan did it; it was fantastic; it was hugely successful but he never made any money. Maria Avino, Arts Trust Founder

"People like Duncan are unsung heroes." Maria Avino

"My job title is 'creative environmental strategic arts analyst' . . . I try to make things happen." Maria Avino

A huge table dominates the long, narrow room.

"Small tables would be far more profitable but we like the big table. People have to sit next to each other and it is a bit of a leveller . . . and, anyhow, it looks good – it suits this room."
Duncan Barlow

"We can **cater** for one to two hundred. We do **celebrations**, we do birthdays, we do wedding receptions, we've done a wake . . . we even did a divorce party . . . and hen nights . . . hen nights are great, but stag nights are **terrible** . . . don't mention **stag nights** – we don't want any more of them." Duncan Barlow

6 We had this great idea that it would all be very **decadent** and bohemian and all the artists would sit round a table and we'd talk about **ideas** . . . but what actually happened was reality set in and the **bills** started to arrive . . . so we had to wake up . . . and that's how the café and the food started . . . it developed out of **necessity**. 9
Maria Avino

Casarecce with Ricotta, Rocket and Basil

serves 4

1 packet casarecce or other tubular pasta
250ml (9fl oz) extra virgin olive oil
salt and coarse black pepper to taste
2 cloves of garlic, sliced finely
100g (3½oz) pine kernels
1 bunch of basil, roughly chopped
1 bunch of rocket, roughly chopped
200g (7oz) ricotta
Parmesan shavings

Cook the pasta in boiling water until al dente. Gently
heat the olive oil and add the salt, pepper, garlic and
pine kernels and cook until the pine kernels are golden
brown. Remove from the heat and add the chopped
basil and rocket. Mix in the ricotta and add the
sauce to the pasta. Serve with Parmesan.

"The whole idea of the place is to give artists the opportunity to exhibit or perform and to provide them with facilities."
Duncan Barlow

Beetroot Borsch with Tarragon Cream

serves 4

1 onion, finely chopped
1 clove of garlic, finely chopped
1 tablespoon vegetable oil
4 heads of beetroot, cooked and peeled
1 litre (1 3/4 pints) vegetable stock
salt and pepper
1 teaspoon dried tarragon
juice of 1 lemon
150ml (1/4 pint) single cream

Add the tarragon and a pinch of salt to the lemon juice and leave to infuse.
Sauté the onion and garlic in hot oil until translucent. Liquidize the onion, garlic
and beetroot along with a small amount of stock. Add the rest of the stock and
return to the heat. Season to taste and simmer for 5-10 minutes. Leave to cool
and then chill. Add the tarragon and lemon juice to the cream and stir
thoroughly. To serve, ladle the soup into a bowl and swirl in some cream.

68

"Candid still has a sense of adventure about it . . . we don't advertize . . . we are difficult
to find . . . you have to walk up a grotty flight of stairs to get here. We don't want to make things
too easy." Maria Avino

The Coffee Gallery

23 Museum Street
London WC1A 0JT

This is a good old-fashioned café. It gives you all the **papers**. I come in here every day on my way to the British Library and have a *civilized* start to the day.
Brian Elliot,
Customer

Tucked away in a small Bloomsbury side street between the British Museum and New Oxford Street, The Coffee Gallery possesses all the attributes of the perfect café: Italian hospitality, bright modern design and excellent food; it is an ideal place to spend a morning poring over the papers with a cappuccino. When Piero and his wife, Henrietta, set up business in a former antique shop in 1991, they had little idea of the success it would bring. Two years after opening The Coffee Gallery, Habitat approached Piero and asked him to run the café at their Kings Road shop. He now heads their catering operations in Dublin and on Tottenham Court Road.

71

The COFFEE gallery

There is no kitchen at The Coffee Gallery; the food is prepared at a central kitchen in New Covent Garden where produce can be bought fresh every day from the vegetable market.

As befits its Bloomsbury location, The Coffee Gallery has a **literary** clientele. Writers, publishers and agents are often to be seen discussing their latest **projects** over lunch.

6 There are lots of **writers** among our regular customers. I've seen **books** started and finished in here. Piero Amodio, Proprietor

74

As its name
implies, The
Coffee Gallery is
more than just a
café. Its walls play
host to regular
monthly
exhibitions by
artists,
photographers
and sculptors. A
selection of
specially imported
southern Italian
ceramics
is constantly on
sale and Henrietta
and Piero are
shortly to expand
their range to
include a selection
of kitchenware.

Pasta with Roasted Tomato and Garlic

serves 4

10 plum tomatoes (preferably San Marzano)
extra virgin olive oil
sea salt
½ bulb of garlic
400g (14oz) short pasta (fusilli, penne etc)
bunch of fresh basil
pepper
freshly grated Parmesan cheese

Pre-heat the oven to 200C (400F/gas mark 6). Place a large pan of water on the burner to heat. Cut the tomatoes into quarters and drizzle with olive oil and sprinkle with sea salt. Place high in the oven to roast for approximately 20 minutes. Gently prize open the ½ garlic bulb, leaving it unpeeled, and drizzle with olive oil. Place it in the oven in a separate dish and roast for the same amount of time as the tomatoes until both are soft and have oozed their natural juices. Coat a pan with olive oil and transfer the tomatoes and garlic to the pan, allowing the garlic cloves to break up. Add a spoonful of olive oil and salt to taste to the pan of water which should now be boiling. Add the pasta and cook until al dente. Tear the basil leaves and stir into the tomato and garlic, adding seasoning to taste. Drain the cooked pasta and mix in the sauce, topping the dish with freshly grated Parmesan cheese.

75

The dishes come from all over **Italy** but they are mostly southern Italian. We use a lot of vegetables. We are 90 per cent **vegetarian**.
Piero Amodio

Piero, a former **photo-journalist**, worked for many years as a war correspondent before giving up travelling and turning to catering in 1977. "I always have a **camera** in my car."
Piero Amodio

Coffee Gallery Fish Cakes

serves 4

300g (10½oz) fresh filleted cod
300g (10½oz) smoked filleted haddock
4 large potatoes
knob of butter
250ml (9fl oz) milk
4 spring onions, chopped
bunch of fresh dill
bunch of fresh flat parsley
salt and pepper
virgin olive oil
1 lemon, cut into wedges

Prepare two pans of boiling water. Gently boil the fish for 10 minutes or until lightly cooked then drain and set aside. Meanwhile, peel and boil the potatoes until soft. Mash the potatoes with the knob of butter and add sufficient milk to make the mash smooth yet still quite dry. Break up the fish into small pieces and mix into the potato along with the spring onion, fresh herbs and salt and pepper. Divide the mixture into 8 portions and shape each into an individual flat fishcake. Fry in hot olive oil until golden and crispy. Drain the fishcakes well and serve with lemon wedges.

Piero ran a number of restaurants before opening The Coffee Gallery, but he prefers the life of a café owner to that of the restaurateur: "I like this sort of environment; at 5.30 we close and I go home . . . there are no problems." Piero Amodio

Carmen, the Café Manager, has worked at The Coffee Gallery for four years. She is never without a smile and a friendly word for her regular customers.

6 The essence of Crowbar is to keep things simple.
No choice ... that's the key to it.
William McLean, Proprietor 9

Crowbar Coffee

55 Exmouth Market
London EC1

Just off Rosebery Avenue at the top of newly-fashionable Farringdon, Crowbar Coffee has distilled the concept of the café down to its bare essence. Its three creators, Samantha Hardingham, William McLean and Adam Sodowick – two architects and a sculptor – have eschewed the clutter associated with a traditional café and gone for space. There are no pictures on the walls, no fussy small tables, no waiter service, no table menus – there is not even any cutlery or crockery; instead the coffee comes in paper cups, the food is served in bags and the short, but excellent, menu is writ large upon the wall.

CROWBAR CAFFEINE CARD

55 Exmouth Market London EC1
MON-FRI 8 - 8

1   2   3

COLLECT 6 STAMPS FOR A FREE COFFEE

4   5   6

William and Adam's original project was a free-standing coffee kiosk but, when no borough councils took up the idea, they teamed up with Samantha and decided to develop the idea for themselves.

"They hated it. They didn't like the idea of encouraging people to hang around on street corners."
Samantha Hardingham, Proprietor

CAFFE MACCH
WATER/NECTA
FRES   ICE
PARM M S
CHOR AN
HA

"We decided to slot the idea into a building rather than having it free-standing."
Adam Sodowick, Proprietor

We don't serve tea . . . *we're a* coffee-bar.

Adam Sodowick

The original Crowbar Coffee opened in a former squat in St John Street in June 1994; the second opened in Exmouth Market in December 1996.

"We're doing urban renewal . . . we get approached by people with really shitty properties in really shitty areas saying, 'Would you like to open a Crowbar?'" Adam Sodowick

"People are always asking to have **exhibitions** on the walls . . . but we only do **events** – no hangings."
Samantha Hardingham

82

6 A lot of it was designed by **catalogue** . . . things that we put together in a way we liked; it is not over-designed. The **stainless steel** cupboards behind the counter for instance: the company that makes them makes them for hospitals; it's a **modular** system. The stools are lab stools and the tables are made from industrial trestles . . . the idea was to keep it as **simple** as possible. **9**
Samantha Hardingham

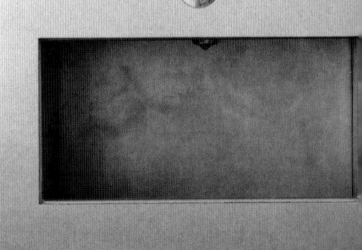

Crowbar Brownies

(created by Pat Lousada – Adam's mother-in-law)

serves 6

300g (10½oz) granulated sugar
3 eggs
70g (2½oz) self-raising flour
40g (1½oz) walnuts, shelled and broken
125g (4½oz) butter
60g (2oz) good cocoa powder

Pre-heat the oven to 190C (375F/gas mark 5). Line a shallow, square baking tin measuring approximately 22 x 22cm (9 x 9in) with greased baking parchment. Whisk the sugar and eggs together then add the sifted flour and walnuts. Melt the butter, stir in the cocoa powder and allow to cool slightly before mixing into the egg and flour mixture. Pour the mixture into the tin and bake for approximately 35 minutes – the brownies are ready when a sharp knife inserted into the baked mixture comes out clean. Allow the brownies to cool for 5 minutes before turning out onto a wire rack to finish cooling.

83

"It is an unaggressive strain of minimalism." Adam Sodowick

Crowbar Chorizo Sandwich

per serving

1 ripe tomato
a few slices of red onion, finely chopped
2–3 fresh basil leaves
extra virgin olive oil
1 whole clove of garlic, crushed
salt and black pepper
1 Portuguese bread roll (available from good Portuguese bakers or Crowbar Coffee)
4 slices Chorizo

Make a salad with the tomato, onion, basil leaves, olive oil and garlic, and season to taste with salt and pepper. Slice the bread roll in two, not cutting completely through so that the two halves are left hinged on one side. Fill the roll with the salad, allowing the juices to soak into the bread. Put a layer of Chorizo on top of the salad and add extra salt and pepper if required. Serve in true Crowbar fashion by wrapping a napkin around its middle.

84

We have two bakers: one Portuguese and one German. We develop some of the recipes which they then make specifically for us. Samantha Hardingham

CYBERIA
CAFE
39 whitfield street
london w1p 5re

Cyberia

39 Whitfield Street
London W1P 5RE

Bright, modern and airy, Cyberia occupies a quiet corner location in Fitzrovia just a stone's throw away from the bustling commercialism of Tottenham Court Road. The menu is limited to an interesting selection of sandwiches, croissants and cakes, because in Cyberia an essential requirement of the food is that it can be prepared quickly and eaten at the keyboard.

87

The digital revolution is happening now – a lot of people believe it is going
to shape our lives in the same way as the motor car. At the moment, I suppose,
we are still walking in front of the car waving a red flag. We have no idea of the
social, economic or cultural dynamics it is going to have in our society,
but it will spread and everybody will be on the Internet like everybody
has got a TV now.

Will Baker, Café Manager

On 1st May 1996, Cyberia played host to the world's first cyberwedding.
The bride and groom made their vows in Fitzrovia; they were connected by video-link to a minister in
Ealing; and their nuptials were broadcast globally on the Internet.

"Next to the computers, the most important aspect of the café is the **coffee**. If anyone asks me if I know the answer to a problem that is too technical, I say 'No . . . but I can make a damn fine **cappuccino**.'
Will Baker

Co-founders, Eva Pascoe and Gené Tiere, were also responsible for setting up the **Women** in Technology Awards. The proportion of women using the computers in Cyberia remains well above **50** per cent.

Not merely a café but a virtual space as well, Cyberia can be visited on the world wide web at **http://www.cyberiacafe.net.**

Cyberia first opened its doors in September 1994, making it the third cybercafé in existence, the first in the UK and possibly the oldest surviving Internet Café in the world.

Chorizo, Gruyère and sundried Tomatoes on Focaccia

per serving

1 portion of Focaccia
extra virgin olive oil
4 slices of Chorizo sausage
2 sundried tomatoes, sliced
2 slices of Gruyère cheese
2 spring onions, chopped
fresh ground pepper
oak leaf lettuce, tomato, chopped spring onions and
black olives to garnish

Split the Focaccia lengthwise and drizzle with oil. Layer
the bottom half of the bread with Chorizo, tomato and
Gruyère. Sprinkle with chopped spring onions and olive oil
and add black pepper to taste. Replace the top half of
the bread and serve with a garnish.

91

Cyberia is staffed not by waiters and waitresses, but by trained cyberhosts who are always on hand to help technophobes take their first tentative steps on the Internet.

Corporate clients can be taught Internet skills over a
cyberbreakfast of coffee and croissant.

Mozzarella, Olives and Salad on Sunflower Bread

per serving

2 slices of sunflower bread
extra virgin olive oil
a few slices of cucumber
a few slices of Mozzarella
1 leaf of oak leaf lettuce
1 tomato, sliced
2 spring onions, coarsely chopped
3 olives, stoned and sliced
salt and fresh ground pepper
oak leaf lettuce, tomato, chopped spring onion and black olives to garnish

Drizzle one slice of bread with olive oil, then layer with cucumber slices,
Mozzarella, oak leaf lettuce and tomato. Sprinkle with chopped spring onions, sliced
olives and olive oil and add salt and pepper to taste. Place the second slice of bread
on top, cut the sandwich into two and serve garnished with a salad of oak leaf
lettuce, tomato, chopped spring onion and black olives.

It's very much a team effort here . . . we are all coming from the same direction.
Matthew Owsley-Brown, Head Chef

The Fifth Floor Café

Harvey Nichols, Knightsbridge
London SW1

As you would expect of London's most fashionable department store, the café at Harvey Nichols is a cut above the rest. In fact, the whole of the fifth floor is turned over to culinary pursuits. In addition to the spacious café, there is a bar, a restaurant and the excellent Foodmarket; it is the ideal place to pause between purchases, rest your feet and carrier bags and mingle with the capital's chicest shopaholics.

95

6 The menus change daily and weekly . . . just depending on what's fresh . . . we're very conscious of what's coming in season . . . for example Jersey Royals and Asparagus are top banana at the moment so they go straight on the menu. 9
Matthew Owsley-Brown

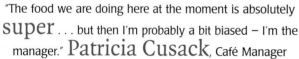

"The food we are doing here at the moment is absolutely super . . . but then I'm probably a bit biased – I'm the manager." Patricia Cusack, Café Manager

"Our Mediterranean menu features some of the best ingredients to be found, reflecting Harvey Nichols' philosophy on quality."
Patricia Cusack

Bright colours, stainless **steel** and space are the order of the day at The Fifth Floor Café. Understatedly-**trendy** waiters and waitresses flit between the tables whilst green-waistcoated staff **churn** out cappuccinos and lattes behind the **bar**.

"It's nice working next to the Foodmarket. If I walk in in the **morning** and think, 'what am I going to put on my menu today?', I can just **wander** through the Foodmarket and get some inspiration." Matthew Owsley-Brown

People don't realize
that catering is very
hard **work**.
Restaurant people
work **hard** and
play hard too . . . it is
very adrenaline
driven – you get a
buzz off it.
Patricia Cusack

The Fifth Floor
Café is also
popular amongst
the **staff** at
Harvey Nichols.

"It's a **great**
place to take
time out
during the day."
**Dietra
Benton**,
Employee

In good weather you can
dine outside – the large,
sunny **terrace** at
Harvey Nichols is a
rarity among central
London cafés.

Fifth Floor Panzanella salad

serves 2

day-old Pane Toscano
    bread (or Ciabatta)
1 red pepper
1 green pepper
1 yellow pepper
a handful of green and
    black olives
8 capers
6 sundried tomatoes
2 cloves of garlic, finely chopped
sea salt to taste
balsamic vinegar
olive oil
parsley, chopped

99

Roast the peppers whole in the oven until they start to blister and blacken, then place in a covered bowl to sweat. When cool, remove the skin and seeds and slice the peppers into strips. Dice the bread into 1cm (½ in) cubes and sprinkle with a little water.

To make the dressing, mix equal proportions of olive oil and balsamic vinegar. Toss all the remaining ingredients together and bind with the dressing (the bread should soak up the dressing and be moist but not too wet). Sprinkle with chopped parsley.

Not only for daytime shoppers, the café, bar and restaurant at Harvey Nichols are open **evenings**. An express **elevator** on Sloane Street and Seville Street **whisks** customers from street level to The Fifth Floor.

Lobster Vol-au-vent

serves 2

225g (8oz) quick puff pastry

225g (8oz) cooked lobster meat

1 carrot, cut into thin rounds

1 courgette, cut into thin rounds

4 baby onions, peeled

1 baby cauliflower, cut into small florettes

1 stem of celery, peeled and sliced on the angle

4 asparagus tips

grain mustard

mayonnaise to bind

chopped chives

chopped parsley

chervil

wild salad leaves

1 egg yolk

Pre-heat the oven to 190C (375F/gas mark 5). To make the vol-au-vent cases, roll out the pastry to 5mm (1/4in) thickness and cut out two rectangles approximately 12.5 x 7.5cm (5 x 3in). Score a smaller rectangle into the surface of each, 5mm (1/4in) in from the outer edge (this will form a rectangular lid which will be lifted out of the centre of the vol-au-vent when cooked). Brush the pastry with egg yolk and bake for 8–10 minutes or until golden.

For the filling, wash all the vegetables, then blanch and quickly refresh the cauliflower, asparagus and onions. Add the grain mustard, chives, parsley and salt and pepper to the mayonnaise to make an intensely-flavoured dressing. Bind the vegetables with the dressing. Remove the lids from the vol-au-vents and fill each pastry case with vegetables. Cut the lobster into chunks, arrange on top of the filling and place the pastry lid on top. Garnish with salad leaves and chervil.

The bottom line is the raw ingredients . . . we're on a crusade for good honest grub.
Matthew Owsley-Brown

Flavoured coffees form a significant part of Hothouse's extensive coffee menu. Café owner, Mel Peters, began importing them five years ago from the Porto Rico Importing Co. in Greenwich Village after a visit to New York, long before they became popular in other London cafés. The rest of the coffees and teas are supplied from owner Mel's home town by Taylors of Harrogate

Hothouse

9 Station Approach
Kew TW9 3QB

Just outside the station in sedate
and leafy Kew, Hothouse is an
oasis of quirkiness and Deco
charm. A wide range of
sandwiches, baked potatoes and
salads form the basis of an
excellent food menu; but it is worth
the trip to Kew alone just to try one
of the monster hot chocolates with
whipped cream, flake and
marshmallows. Housed in the
former Kew Post Office building,
traces of Hothouse's institutional
origins can still be seen in the
industrial-sized central heating and
the bars on the windows.

"We remember it when it used to be a **Post Office**. We still come in here to post our **letters** and wonder what happened." **Clare Simpson,** Customer

Having just come back from **travelling**, I have to say that I never found a **mocha** as good as here. **Elaine Vanner,** Customer

Trained as a chartered accountant, Mel Peters gave up her job in Soho to pursue her long-standing ambition of running a café. "The decision was a spur of the moment thing; mind you, being an accountant helps with the business side of things."
Melanie Peters, Proprietor

Hothouse was converted from its former glory as a Post Office by Mel, her brother, mother and boyfriend, Scott Ackroyd. Scott is also responsible for the menus which have proved so attractive to customers that, in summer, they have to be chained to the outdoor tables to prevent them from being pinched.

People think that running a café is fun; that it is all sitting around and talking to customers . . . actually it is really hard work.
Mel Peters

The walls of Hothouse are regularly adorned with **weird** and wonderful **art** works by local artists.

"We try to keep away from flowery type things. We had some huge **life drawings**, but we had to take them down – they **disturbed** some of the **customers**."

Mel Peters

When Hothouse opened for business in 1991, some of the more **elderly** residents of Kew **blamed** them for closing the Post Office down.

Bean soup

serves 6

4 tablespoons olive oil
1 large onion, finely chopped
3 cloves of garlic, finely sliced
2 sticks of celery, finely chopped
2 x 425g (15oz) tins of chopped tomatoes
2 tablespoons tomato purée
2 tablespoons tomato ketchup
2 vegetable stock cubes
2 bay leaves
½ teaspoon vegetable extract
1 teaspoon Worcester sauce
dash of tabasco sauce
1 teaspoon honey
salt and pepper to taste
425g (15oz) tin of flageolet beans, drained
425g (15oz) tin of butter beans, drained
425g (15oz) tin of cannellini beans, drained
    (or 3 tins of your own preferred choice of beans)
3 tablespoons chopped parsley
3 tablespoons chopped fresh basil

sauté the onion until softened and then add the garlic and
celery and cook for a further 4–5 minutes. Add the rest of the
ingredients except the beans, parsley and basil and simmer for
10–15 minutes. Add the beans, herbs and generous amounts of
salt and pepper. Gradually add approximately ½ pint of water
(or to your preferred consistency) and simmer until the beans
are warmed through. serve with fresh, crusty bread.

Avocado, Bacon and Gruyère salad with Croûtons

serves 4

salad

4 slices of Ciabatta, cut into 1cm (½ in) cubes

olive oil

selection of washed salad leaves: half an iceberg lettuce; whole head of oak leaf
    lettuce; handful of raddichio leaves; or other fancy lettuce of your choice

2 avocados, stoned and diced

8 rashers of bacon, grilled and chopped

175g (6oz) Gruyère cheese, diced into 1cm (½ in) cubes

Dressing

9 tablespoons extra virgin olive oil

3 tablespoons white wine vinegar

½–1 teaspoon runny honey

1 tablespoon whole grain mustard

1 clove of garlic, crushed

juice of ½ lemon

salt and pepper

Fry the cubed bread in olive oil until golden brown. Drain and place on kitchen
paper. Place all the ingredients for the salad dressing in a screw top jar and shake
vigorously until thoroughly blended. Place the mixed leaves in a bowl and toss
together. Add the avocado, bacon, Gruyère and croûtons and pour on the salad
dressing. serve with Ciabatta bread.

Hothouse is strangely popular with athletes. Both Linford Christie
and Colin Jackson are regular customers of Hothouse and both have
praised Mel's speciality sandwiches in the pages of *Esquire* magazine.

Konditor, *m.* (**-s,** *pl* **-en**) pastry-cook, confectioner. **Konditorei**, *f.* confectioner's shop. **Konditoreiwaren,** *pl.* confectioner.

Konditor
& Cook

66 The Cut
London SE1 8LZ

South of the river, five minutes
from the bustle of Waterloo
Station and the concrete edifices
of the South Bank, Konditor &
Cook occupies a stylish and
minimal space next to The Young
Vic theatre. In the evening it
serves as the theatre bar while
during the day the staff of
Konditor & Cook concentrate on
what they do best: serving high
quality food in a relaxing,
modern environment.

To create a space that is your own is a pure form of self-expression.

Mark Ryan,
Café Manager

Konditor & Cook was a finalist in the *Best Budget Meal* category of the 1996 *Time Out* Eating and Drinking Awards.

Given its **central** position in South London's theatrical square mile, it is not surprising that Konditor & Cook's clientele has a strong thespian element. In the morning **actors** and theatre staff linger over cappuccinos and pastries or treat themselves to a cooked breakfast, while at lunch time the café **buzzes** with customers drawn in from further afield by the midday menu.

Konditor & Cook's chef, **Curtis Youé**, is an ex-punk-rock bass guitarist who traded in his guitar to pursue a creative career in the kitchen.

We all have a past; catering is the poor man's **foreign legion** *. . . you go into catering to* **forget***.*
Mark Ryan

Elemental materials

have been employed in the design of both the café and the bakery. In the café, natural oak is contrasted with galvanized steel seating and concrete while in the bakery, use is made of black granite and stainless steel. This notion is reflected in the food; simple high-quality ingredients are combined with considerable flair to create an imaginative and varied modern European

menu.

Konditor, Gerhard Jenne, uses only **free-range** eggs and quality butter in all of his baking. He specializes in **one-off** commissions and has created cakes for Mick Jagger, Tina Turner, Jerry Hall and Ringo Starr.

Potato Cakes with Smoked Salmon   serves 4

Potato Cakes
800g (1lb 2oz) potatoes
spring onion, finely chopped
20g (1oz) butter
nutmeg, salt and pepper to taste
oil for frying

Lemon Dressing
juice and zest of 2 lemons
1 tablespoon wholegrain mustard
150ml (1/4 pint) olive oil
salt, pepper and caster sugar to taste

Salad
1 plum, halved and sliced
1 pear, quartered and sliced
2 strawberries, sliced
4 cherry tomatoes, quartered
1/2 cucumber, sliced
1 large curly endive
+
150g (5 1/2 oz) red cabbage, grated
150g (5 1/2 oz) fromage frais
250g (9oz) Scottish smoked salmon
1/2 bunch of chives, chopped

Boil the potatoes for 20 minutes, drain and mash them, adding the spring onion, butter, nutmeg and seasoning to taste. Allow to cool, preferably overnight. Arrange the plums, pears, strawberries, tomato and cucumber alternately in a ring around the outside of each plate. Place an inner ring of curly endive in the shape of a nest. Pour the ingredients for the lemon dressing into a sealed jar and shake until thoroughly blended. Shape the cold mash into four patties and fry in a little hot oil for 3-4 minutes on each side until golden. Place a hot potato cake in the centre of each plate and encircle with grated red cabbage. Drizzle the lemon dressing onto the salad, then top each potato cake with fromage frais then smoked salmon. Decorate with a sprinkling of chopped chives.

Gerhard Jenne, Proprietor of Konditor & Cook
by Ann Gardner

Konditor & Cook

Gerhard Jenne, not just a Konditor but a Konditor Meister, established the Konditor & Cook bakery in Cornwall Road in 1993. Demand for his quality baking was so high and requests for a space in which to sit and enjoy his excellent cooking were so frequent, that when the space became available in August 1995, Konditor & Cook took over the café at The Young Vic theatre.

Minted Tabbouleh serves 4

Tabbouleh
400g (14oz) bulgar wheat
1 cucumber
1 red pepper, de-seeded and diced
2 spring onions, finely chopped
bunch fresh mint, finely chopped
60ml (2fl oz) lemon juice
120ml (4fl oz) olive oil
salt and pepper

Red Pepper Sauce
2 red peppers, quartered and de-seeded
4 tablespoons sunflower oil
60ml (2fl oz) red wine
100g (3½oz) onions, chopped
1 clove of garlic, chopped
+
200g (7oz) curd cheese
mixed salad leaves, cherry tomatoes and
4 sprigs of mint to garnish

Pre-heat the oven to 200C (400F/gas mark 6). Soak the bulgar wheat in twice the volume of boiling water until soft to the bite (approximately 20 minutes). Rinse under cold water, drain and refrigerate. Cut 8 slices of cucumber to save as garnish and peel, de-seed and dice the remainder of the cucumber. Mix the chopped cucumber, pepper, spring onion and mint into the bulgar wheat along with the lemon juice, olive oil and salt and pepper to taste. Store in the refrigerator.

To make the pepper sauce, place the pepper quarters on a roasting tray, drizzle with 2 tablespoons of oil and roast for 30 minutes then allow to cool. Sauté the onion and garlic in the remaining oil over a low heat until soft. Add the red wine and simmer for 5 minutes. Mix all the sauce ingredients together and blend until smooth. Pass the sauce through a sieve, season to taste and chill.

To serve, press a portion of tabbouleh into a bowl and turn it out in the centre of a plate. Pour red pepper sauce around it. Lay a garnish of mixed leaves, 2 slices of cucumber and a cherry tomato at one side of each plate. Using two tablespoons, shape the curd cheese into quenelles and place two on each plate opposite the salad. Finish with a sprig of mint.

> Simple things well done – that is our philosophy.
> **Mark Ryan**, Café Manager

Maison Bertaux

28 Greek Street
London W1B 5LL

Sandwiched between a peep show and the famous Coach and Horses pub at the bottom of Greek Street, Maison Bertaux is a Soho landmark. Serving the best in Soho cakes and keeping to a tradition that is resolutely French – there is no Gaggia machine on display here. Its Welsh-French owner, Michelle Wade, continues to run the café in flamboyant style. Its intimate, faded interior is dearly loved by customers and staff alike.

Maison Bertaux was originally founded in 1871 by a member of the Communards who escaped from Paris.

"It is difficult to find a café that is this old-fashioned in this economic climate."
Michelle Wade, Proprietor

119

"I like it to be a bit like a **sitting room** ... so it's like coming into someone's house."
Michelle Wade

6 I'm in love with this place. I started here as a **Saturday** girl when I was fourteen . . . I've got so used to it, it's gone into my blood. Michelle Wade, Proprietor 9

121

"She's Welsh-French . . . it's a potent combination, I tell you." Pickles, Customer

"She cries at the drop of a hat . . . it's RADA, I tell you." Pickles

6 I like being upset . . . what's a day without being upset for goodness sake. Michelle Wade 9

The small upstairs tea room doubles as a theatre for the Maison Bertaux Theatre Club who put on regular productions of both Shakespeare and contemporary drama. "All the tables are taken out and the chairs are put in rows. It seats twenty people and that's it." Michelle Wade

Mont Blanc

makes 12–15

<u>Meringue</u>
6 egg whites
350g (12oz) caster sugar

<u>Topping</u>
1 small tin chestnut spread
1 tablespoon rum
25g (1oz) icing sugar
300ml (½ pint) whipping cream
25g (1oz) caster sugar
whipped cream to decorate

"When it is hot we just bake the **minimum** . . . there is no point in having it there and not selling it."
Michelle Wade

123

Pre-heat the oven to 150C (300F/gas mark 2). To make the meringue bases, whisk the egg whites and 225g (8oz) of the caster sugar together until it forms stiff peaks. Add the remaining sugar and whisk for a further 30 seconds. Pipe or spoon ovals of the mixture onto a baking tray lined with grease-proof paper and bake for 1 hour.

To make the filling, beat the chestnut spread, rum and icing sugar together until smooth. Whip the cream and the caster sugar together and gently fold it into the mixture. Pipe the mixture onto the cooled meringue bases and decorate with squiggles of fresh whipped cream.

Raspberry Barquette   makes 12

Sweet Pastry
175g (6oz) butter
250g (9oz) plain flour
80g (3oz) caster sugar
1 egg

+

1 punnet of raspberries
icing sugar to decorate

Crème Patisserie
1 pint milk
1/4 vanilla pod or 2 drops of vanilla essence
120g (4oz) caster sugar
4 egg yolks
80g (3oz) plain flour
1 tablespoon rum
2 tablespoons whipped cream

Pre-heat the oven to 180C (350F/gas mark 4). To make the sweet pastry, cut the butter into small pieces and rub it into the flour until the mixture resembles breadcrumbs. Beat the egg and sugar together and mix into the flour mixture. Knead the pastry until it is smooth and chill for at least 30 minutes. Roll out the pastry until it is approximately 5mm (1/4 in) thick. Line 12 boat-shaped moulds with the pastry, prick with a fork and bake for 15-20 minutes.

To make the crème patisserie, gently heat the milk together with the vanilla in a small pan. In a separate bowl, whisk the sugar and egg yolks together until pale in colour. Sieve the flour and gradually add it to the egg to form a stiff paste. Just before it comes to the boil, stir a little milk into the egg mixture. As the milk comes to the boil, add the egg mixture and cook for 1 minute, stirring continuously until thickened. Pour the crème into a dish, cover the surface with buttered grease-proof paper to prevent a skin forming and leave to cool. Whisk the cold crème patisserie, add the rum and fold in the whipped cream. Pipe the crème into the pastry boats, arrange the raspberries on top and dust with icing sugar.

The recipes are secret . . . I keep them in a safe downstairs. And that is why I keep all my staff; they can really misbehave but I can't afford to let them leave.
Michelle Wade

THE NOTED EEL & PIE HOUSES

87 Tower Bridge Road
London S.E.1
Tel: 071-407 2985

105 Peckham High Street
London S.E.15
Tel: 071-277 6181

M. Manze

87 Tower Bridge Road
London SE1 4TW

It might be a simple formula – meat pies, eels (jellied or stewed), liquor and mash – but it remains perennially popular among the wide boys and thin girls of East London, and there is nowhere better to sample the capital's original fast food than at M. Manze on Tower Bridge Road. Here, at London's oldest surviving eel and pie house, cheerful, green-uniformed staff serve up traditional London fare in an environment that has barely changed in a century.

INSIDE PRICES

1 PIE & LIQUOR
1 PIE 1 MASH
1 PIE 2 MASH
2 PIE 1 MASH
2 PIE 2 MASH
EELS & MASH
JELLIED EELS
PIES EXTRA
MASH EXTRA
COLD DRINKS
TEA 45 COFFEE
PIE TAKE AWAY

The pies are still made to the original recipe. They are prepared from scratch each morning and delivered fresh to the waiting staff by dumb waiter from the bakery below.

The Bermondsey shop was originally established by Robert Cooke in 1892. It became a Manze's in 1902 when Michele Manze, who ran the ice merchant's and confectioner's next door, fell in love with and married Robert Cooke's daughter.

PIES EXTRA 60
MASH EXTRA 95
50

TAKE AWAY

PIES 85
MASH 50
LIQUOR 45 75
STEWED EELS 1 65
JELLIED 1 65

A true family business,
M. Manze is now owned and
run by Michele Manze's three
grandsons:
Graham, Geoffrey
and Richard Poole.

The Tower Bridge Road shop was the first in the Manze dynasty. By the end of the 1930s, there were fourteen shops across London bearing the Manze name.

The perfectly preserved interior is understandably popular with photographers and film makers; it has featured in an Elton John video and has been used for a variety of fashion shoots.

We keep to the old methods; as well as the old ingredients, we stick to the old machinery – our pastry-rolling machine dates from 1928. We use them because they are made of cast iron . . . the new machines can't take the hammering.

Geoffrey Poole, Proprietor

Stewed Eels in Parsley Sauce

per serving

5 or 6 pieces of eel (preferably English)
small knob of butter
salt and pepper
1 dessertspoon plain flour
75ml (3fl oz) milk, mixed with 200ml (7fl oz) water
1 large sprig of parsley, chopped

Bring ½ pint of salted water to the boil and add the eels.
Reduce the heat to a gentle simmer. Skim off any surface
matter and simmer for approximately 10 minutes until the
flesh comes cleanly away from the bone when pressed.
While the eels are cooking, melt the butter in a saucepan and
stir in the flour to form a roux. Season with salt and pepper
and the milk and water and bring gently to the boil, stirring
continuously, until the sauce thickens.
When the sauce has thickened, add the parsley and cook for a
further 2 minutes. Strain the eels and add to the sauce. Serve
with mashed potatoes.

131

M. Manze has a sister shop at 105 High Street Peckham, SE15. It was burnt out in the
riots of 1985 but re-opened in 1990, after a long legal battle with Southwark Council.

Traditional Minced Beef Pie

It is not possible to emulate a traditional pie-shop pie
in a domestic oven, but this recipe is a good alternative.

2 tablespoons plain flour
225g (8oz) lean minced beef
oil
¼ onion, chopped
½ pint beef stock
salt and pepper
212g (7½ oz) packet of puff pastry
milk to glaze

Pre-heat the oven to 200C (400F/ gas mark 6). Put the flour into a large plastic
bag, add the mince and shake well until thoroughly coated. Heat a frying pan
with a little oil and sauté the onion. Add the mince and fry until just brown.
Pour in the beef stock and add salt and pepper to taste. Stir and simmer for 3
minutes. Roll out half the pastry and line a suitably-sized greased pie dish. Pour
the filling into the pastry-lined dish and dampen the edges of the pastry. Roll out
the other half of the pastry and completely cover the filling, pressing down the
edges to seal. Trim the excess pastry from around the dish using a blunt knife
and brush the top of the pie with milk. Make a slit in the top of the pie to let
out steam. Bake in the oven for approximately 20 minutes or until golden brown.
Serve in the traditional pie shop fashion with mashed potatoes and parsley sauce.

6 These are the best pies in the country.
I've been coming here since I was eighteen . . .
I'm even shaped like a pie.
Levi Lee, Customer 9

Anyone who is anyone in the East End has eaten at Pellicci's. Ask to see Tony's autograph book; it is nearly as impressive as his Elvis impersonation.

Pellicci's most infamous customers were the Kray brothers. "They were always perfectly respectful . . . they used to tell the other customers off for swearing." Nevio Pellicci, Proprietor

E. Pellicci

332 Bethnal Green Road
London E2

E. Pellicci on Bethnal Green Road is the most exquisite example of an Italian caff in London. The food comes in generous portions, the hospitality is unswerving and the detailed marquetry-work interior is more reminiscent of a Pullman Carriage than an East End café. Whether you are a regular or are visiting for the first time, you are always assured a friendly welcome at E. Pellicci.

135

The framed bag above the counter is the only one left of 25,000 printed for the Coronation in 1953.

"Collis along the road here said I've served five generations of his family . . . I said, 'leave off' . . . but it's true . . . I remember his grandfather, his father, him, his daughter and little Oliver. I know I'm getting on but that's ridiculous." Nevio Pellicci

My mother used to wash up the cups here until she was eighty-six. We've had loads of other people come and do it since but nobody can do it like my mum.
Nevio Pellicci

Without a mobile phone you are underdressed at Pellicci's.

The magnificent marquetry work was done a bit at a time in 1946 by Achille Cappocci, an Italian craftsman whose workshop was just around the corner.

In those days there used to be a lot of **cabinet makers** in Bethnal Green. All these local chaps that knew about furniture would come in and say, 'I bet **Cappocci's** done that.' They all knew that Cappocci was **number one**.

Nevio Pellicci

Nevio's father originally started work in the café making the ice cream. He took it over in 1915 and it has been in the family ever since. Nevio was born in the flat upstairs and his wife, Maria; his children, Anna and Nevio Junior; and his nephew, Tony, now work in the café.

6 Pellicci's famous bread pudding is made to a secret recipe handed down from Nevio's mother to his wife Maria. Take my word for it, you'll never have tasted bread pudding like this . . . I can't give you the recipe for that one – that's too good that one . . . and even if Maria told you what to do, it still wouldn't come out the same. 9

Nevio Pellicci

The chips at Pellicci's are famed throughout the East End. Each one is hand cut by Maria. "There's a Crypto machine out the back but Maria won't use it." Nevio Pellicci

special Breast of Chicken

serves 4

2 cloves of garlic, chopped finely
bunch of fresh parsley, chopped
few sprigs of fresh basil, chopped
dried mixed herbs
4 chicken breasts
salt and pepper

Mix the garlic, fresh herbs and dried herbs together
and sprinkle onto a baking tray. Flatten the chicken
breasts and press them into the herbs, coating them
thoroughly. season with salt and pepper and leave
overnight to absorb the flavours. Cook the chicken
under a very hot grill for 2-3 minutes either side or
until cooked through and serve with a selection of
vegetables.

Traditional Lasagne

serves 6

Bolognese sauce
1 tablespoon olive oil
1 small onion, chopped
1 stick celery, chopped
1 clove of garlic, crushed
1kg (2lb 4oz) minced beef
425g (15oz) tin of tomatoes
1 tablespoon tomato purée
2 leaves of fresh basil, finely chopped
2 bay leaves
salt and pepper
a pinch of nutmeg

Béchamel sauce
60g (2oz) butter
60g (2oz) plain flour
600ml (1 pint) milk
2 tablespoons Parmesan cheese, grated
a pinch of nutmeg
salt and pepper

+

8 sheets of lasagne

Pre-heat the oven to 180C (350F/gas mark 4). To make the Bolognese sauce, heat the oil in a pan and sauté the onion, celery and garlic. Add the minced beef and, when the beef is browned, add the tinned tomatoes, tomato purée and herbs. Bring to the boil, add 1 pint of water and season with salt, pepper and nutmeg. Simmer for about 1 hour until the sauce has thickened. Remove the bay leaves. For the Béchamel sauce, melt the butter in a pan, add the flour to make a roux and gradually stir in the milk. Stir continuously until the sauce thickens and then add the cheese, nutmeg and salt and pepper.
Boil the lasagne in salted boiling water. Pour alternate layers of Bolognese sauce and Béchamel sauce into a cooking dish, separating each with a layer of pasta, starting with a layer of Bolognese sauce and finishing with a layer of Béchamel sauce. Bake for 1 hour.

"We get a lot of people from the gym round the corner . . .
they just eat a bowl of rice or a bowl of pasta . . . although
it's usually accompanied by steak, chicken or liver." Nevio Pellicci

For the serious poetry lover, a wide range of books and periodicals are on sale at The Poetry Place including The Poetry Society's own best-selling magazine, *The Poetry Review*.

The Poetry Place

22 Betterton Street
London WC2H 9BU

The Poetry Place – the café of the Poetry Society – is a tranquil, literary refuge just around the corner from the bustling commercialism of Covent Garden. It is the perfect place to pore over verse; whether you choose to ensconce yourself in an armchair in the cosy basement reading-room or sit at one of the elegant tables on the ground floor. Annual café membership costs just £3.00 and includes a copy of the Poetry Society Newsletter.

143

Words are taken very seriously at the poetry place.
A magnetic poetry kit is available to any customers
who feel the creative urge and, at one point, they even
contemplated putting alphabetti spaghetti
on the menu.

6 We were thinking about having
T.S.Eliot coffee spoons . . .
to measure out your life.
Clare Elwes, Café Manager 9

"We want people to think they can sit
here and play scrabble for a
couple of hours . . . you shouldn't
feel like you have to drink your coffee
and leave." Clare Elwes

The **handsome tables** and extraordinary Ralph Steadman **lamp shades** at The Poetry Place were designed and made by **David Murphy**. The tables themselves were individually **sponsored** by various **publishers**.

The Poetry Society was one of the first beneficiaries of the **National Lottery**. The money was used to convert the reading-room and basement into what is now The Poetry Place.

Regular poetry events are all part of The Poetry Place philosophy; there are readings, poetry cabaret and, every Tuesday, Poetry Unplugged – a popular open-mike night hosted by John Citizen.

146

'It went on till nearly **midnight** the other night . . . nearly four and a half hours . . . I can't listen to anything – even **Bruce Springsteen** – for four and a half hours.' John Citizen, Poet

"You can sign up and read or just turn up and watch." John Citizen

Café Society

Eat in or take away.

On the go al fresco.

Mobile phone anxiety,

No sugar piety.

Espresso plotted coups,

Table waiting queues.

Froth without sediment,

Tables without condiment.

Starters that don't,

Desserts that won't.

Food to die for,

Food to diet for.

And when you

Have digested

The menu,

Could I see it please.

But firstly, two teas?

147

© John Citizen 1997

Tomato and Orange Soup with Oat Cakes *serves 2-3*

Soup
1 onion, chopped
1 litre (1¾ pint) stock
900g (2lb) tomatoes
salt and black pepper
bay leaf
zest and juice of 1 orange
75ml (3fl oz) single cream
chopped parsley to garnish

Oat cakes (makes 12)
225g (8oz) medium oatmeal
1 teaspoon sea salt
¼ teaspoon bicarbonate of soda
50g (2oz) butter

To make the soup, gently sauté the onion until it is soft then add the stock and tomatoes. Season well with salt, black pepper and a bay leaf. Partially cover and leave to cook over a gentle heat for about 15 minutes until the tomatoes are soft. Remove from the heat, liquidize the soup and then return to the heat and add the orange zest and juice. Gently blend the cream into the soup and heat to thicken but do not allow to boil. Serve with a little chopped parsley.

To make the oat cakes, pre-heat the oven to 190C (357F/gas mark 5). Boil 8 tablespoons of water in a small saucepan and add the butter and heat until it melts. Mix all the dry ingredients in a bowl and stir the butter and water into the oatmeal to make a soft dough — if necessary, add a little extra oatmeal to make the dough easy to handle. Form the dough into a ball and press it flat on a pastry board sprinkled with a little oatmeal until it is approximately 5mm (¼in) thick. Cut out rounds using a plain pastry cutter or an upturned glass, place on a baking sheet sprinkled with oatmeal and bake in the middle of the oven for 25-30 minutes. Cool on a rack and store in an air tight container.

The menu, devised by chef and **documentary** film maker **Jessica York**, is a pleasing combination of light lunches and traditional English tea-time food such as ginger buns, crumpets and anchovy toast.

Before Highgate village was absorbed into London's metropolitan sprawl in the late nineteenth century, The Raj Tea Room was originally a farmhouse. A secret tunnel is still rumoured to connect the cellar of The Raj with the crypt of the church opposite.

The Raj Tea Room is only a five minute walk from Hampstead Heath.

"Our Clientele? I call them the 'welligog people': people who don't mind being seen in a pair of wellingtons; that type of person."
D'arcy Brewester, Proprietor

The Raj
Tea Room

67 Highgate High Street
London N6 5JX

Occupying the first floor of a Queen Anne house in the heart of picturesque Highgate, The Raj Tea Room was founded in 1978 by D'arcy Brewester. Passionately adverse to fast food, D'arcy brought the principle of refectory living with him from his colonial Indian childhood. Substantial portions of hearty food, including a variety of Anglo-Indian curries, are served at large tables in an intimate and informal atmosphere.

6 It doesn't cost any more to give
you an extra potato, an extra carrot and
an extra onion.
Our motto is,
Wagamama who? 9
D'arcy Brewester

"All my life I've wanted a **dog** that sits under tables . . . and now I've got one; that's one **achievement**." D'arcy Brewester

From **poetry** readings to Moroccan drummers, regular entertainment evenings are another aspect of The Raj's **informal** philosophy.

"He's called **Barking Lord Scruff** of Highgate. There's a good reason for that – he barks, he is a lord, he's scruffy and he **lives** in Highgate." D'arcy Brewester

I have this dream *of being at the vanguard of* cottage *industry. We've gone too far with factory-made stuff. 90 per cent of what we do here is either made by us or from a tiny* specialist *firm.*

D'arcy Brewester

When not in use as a café, the relaxed surroundings of The Raj double as D'arcy's living room.

The Raj started life as a tea room but rapidly **progressed** to providing lunches and evening meals. The premises are now shared with an independent **clothes designer**, a traditional clockmaker and D'arcy's own bed and breakfast.

Quick Cassoulet de Carcassonne

serves 4

Cassoulet de Carcassonne is a dish that was developed during the siege of Carcassonne. The French town was on the point of starvation and so the mayor ordered a large cooking pot to be placed in the town square. The pot was filled with whatever remaining foodstuffs the inhabitants could find and these ingredients, of which rat formed a major part, were slow cooked for days over a low flame to create a nourishing stew. D'arcy's quick version makes use of a wok instead of a cassoulet and chicken is substituted for the traditional rat.

1 tablespoon vegetable oil
4 beef sausages, chopped into 1cm (½ in) sections
4 rashers of bacon, roughly chopped
1 large chicken breast, cut into chunks
1 large onion, roughly chopped
1 red pepper, de-seeded and chopped into strips
½ teaspoon mixed herbs
¼ small white cabbage, shredded
425g (15oz) tin Haricot beans or butter beans
150ml (¼ pint) vegetable stock
3 medium potatoes, boiled and cubed
60ml (2¼fl oz) milk
salt and fresh ground pepper

Heat the vegetable oil in a wok or heavy-based pan and fry the sausage, bacon and chicken for 2–3 minutes. Add the chopped onion and red pepper and continue frying for 5 minutes until the onion is translucent. Stir in the mixed herbs, cabbage, beans (including the fluid) and stock. Simmer for 5 minutes and then add the potato cubes, milk and salt and pepper to taste. Cook for a further 5 minutes and serve either on a bed of rice or with bread.

Given the reasonable prices, it is no surprise that Tadim is popular with students from the neighbouring art college; a filling meal of borek and salad at Tadim will set you back only £2.00.

Tadim Café

41 Camberwell Church Street
London SE5 8TR

Just around the corner from
Camberwell Green in South London,
is one of the capital's best kept
secrets. From the front Tadim Café
may look like a normal Turkish café
but, walk past the stacked trays of
borek and baclava and spend some
time in the charming sunny
courtyard at the rear and you will
find yourself picking up travel
brochures on the way home.

159

Sener Saglam, the owner and head pastry chef, would like to dedicate more of his time to creating patisserie, but the traditional **Turkish pastries** are popular with his customers and he is such a perfectionist that he refuses to delegate responsibility.

It's the best baclava I have ever had – it's really moist; but you have to eat it in one mouthful. I bit into the first one and dripped honey all over the floorboards. Alex Frith, Customer

Food at Tadim is not limited to traditional Turkish fare. Sener Saglam, a **master** pastry chef, also bakes a wide range of croissants, Danish pastries and cakes.

 161

For those not **tempted** by the traditional Turkish dishes, Tadim serves a wide range of **sandwiches**.

Sener Saglam has wanted to be a pastry chef since he was **six**. He started work **washing up** in a café before becoming **apprenticed** to the chef.

6 This place is my **life**. I love this place; they are like my **family**. If I leave this job it is to go back to my country for good. **Nina**, Waitress 9

The cheerful **international** staff at Tadim exemplify the café motto: '**Love** all and **serve** all'.

Coffee comes in many variations at Tadim: cappuccino, espresso, **latte** and, of course, **Turkish**

Lahmacun (traditional Turkish pizza)

serves 6

Base
450g (1lb) strong white
    flour
1 teaspoon olive oil
pinch of salt
1 teaspoon easy blend yeast

Topping
225g (½lb) minced lamb
1 medium onion, chopped
1 small green pepper, chopped
350g (¾lb) tomatoes,
    puréed
small bunch of parsley,
    chopped
½ teaspoon salt
ground pepper
1 teaspoon olive oil

Pre-heat the oven to 240C (475F/gas mark 9). To make the base, sieve the flour
into a large mixing bowl. Mix in the yeast, add the oil and salt and slowly stir
in ½ pint of water until it forms an elastic dough. Knead the dough thoroughly
and put to one side.

To make the topping, stir all the ingredients together. Roll the dough out thinly
and cut out six 20cm (8in) circles. Spread a handful of the topping onto each
base, press it down firmly and bake for 5–6 minutes. Serve rolled in tubes and
stuffed with salad.

Spinach and Feta Borek

serves 6

1 large onion, chopped finely
1 tablespoon olive oil
200g (7oz) fresh spinach, chopped
2 eggs
150ml (¼ pint) milk
25g (1oz) semolina
200g (7oz) feta cheese
680g (1lb 8oz) puff pastry

Pre-heat the oven to 190C (375F/gas mark 5). Sauté the onion in the olive oil until translucent, then add the spinach and salt and pepper to taste. Mix in one egg and leave to cool. Meanwhile boil the milk, add the semolina and a little pepper and stir. When it thickens, add an egg, crumble in the feta cheese and remove from the heat. Stir the semolina mixture into the onion and spinach to create the filling. Roll out the puff pastry and cut it into six 15cm (6in) squares. Place a spoonful of the filling in the centre of each square of pastry, fold over to form a triangular parcel and seal by dampening the edges. Bake for approximately 30 minutes or until browned.

6 Clapham is a
schizophrenic
area . . . the High Street is
really working class but the
rest of it is so posh . . .
for people who can't afford
to live in Chelsea.
Richard Kelly,
Proprietor 9

Tea Time

21 The Pavement
London SW4 0HY

Just a short walk from Clapham
Common station, Tea Time is a
pink-tableclothed time-warp to the
1950s. Sedate, civilized and
charming, this quintessentially
English tea shop occupies two
floors of a former hairdresser's
opposite the Common. There is
nowhere better to gorge yourself on
home-made cakes or feast on
splendid all-day breakfasts of
creamy scrambled eggs and
smoked salmon.

167

Richard Kelly, who rather ironically doesn't drink tea, took over Tea Time from the original owners in 1992.

We decorated it all; it was just plain green before; a bit boring. We wanted it to look like a run-down bed and breakfast at the seaside with a bit of character . . . or like your aunt's front room.

Richard Kelly

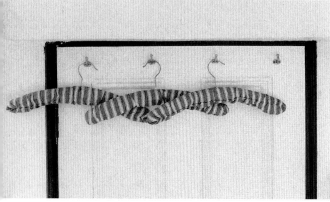

From Darjeeling to Assam, Tea Time stocks an extensive range of teas – all fine quality loose leaf and served by the pot. For those not attracted to tannin, there is also a range of herbal infusions

Tea Time has its own blend of tea, specially made up by Cawardines. Earl Grey, however, is most popular amongst the customers.

The quaint downstairs room at Tea Time is available for private functions. On one occasion they had three DJs from *The Fridge* playing there.

Whole cakes are available to take away from the counter at the front of the shop.

If you prefer your cake al fresco, Tea Time can make up a picnic box to take onto the common

The Grafton

per serving

Scottish smoked salmon
3 slices of granary bread, buttered
cucumber, sliced
mayonnaise
½ avocado, stoned and sliced
prawns
lemon, cucumber, orange, tomato, cress and
*   strawberries to garnish*

*Place a generous helping of smoked salmon on
the first slice of bread and top with
cucumber. Place the next slice of bread on
top and spread with mayonnaise. Sprinkle
prawns on top and then add a layer of
avocado. Cover with the final slice of bread
and cut the sandwich into four. Arrange
the sandwiches on a plate and garnish.*

> The Grafton is named after a posh square round the corner.
> Richard Kelly

Tea Time is not **just** for afternoon tea. In addition to the excellent cakes, they serve a range of substantial speciality **breakfasts** and a wide variety of **sandwiches**

Banoffi Pie

serves 8–12

500g (1lb 2oz) packet of digestive biscuits, crushed
200g (7oz) butter, melted
2 tins of condensed milk
5 ripe bananas
300ml (½ pint) orange juice
1 teaspoon cinnamon
600ml (1 pint) double cream
grated chocolate to decorate

Mix the crushed biscuits and melted butter and press the mixture into a 23cm (9in) cake tray. Boil the unopened cans of milk in water for at least 3 hours, topping up the water from time to time to ensure that the pan does not boil dry. Allow to cool, open the cans and spread the resulting caramel over the biscuit base. Slice the bananas and soak them in the orange juice and cinnamon. Layer the bananas over the toffee. Whisk the cream until stiff and smooth over the bananas. Sprinkle with grated chocolate.

Have you tried our **cheesecake**? It is lovely. I'm not going to give you the recipe for that!
Richard Kelly, Proprietor

Troubadour *n*. Lyric poet in S. France etc. 11th-13th c., singing in Provencal mainly of chivalry and courtly love. [F, f. Prov. trobador (trobar find, invent, compose in verse)]

Troubadour

239 Old Brompton Road
London SW5

Just five minutes from Earls Court
station, Troubadour is the closest it
is possible to find to a traditional
eighteenth-century London coffee-
house. The walls are dark, the coffee
strong, the music baroque and the
atmosphere conducive to creativity
and the exchange of ideas.

"They do say about the Troubadour that
you can check out but you can never
leave."

Isabella Meaden-
Barber, Chef

176

Shunning modernity and current fads, Troubadour remains resolutely as it was at the beginning of the **1960s**. When Troubadour was **renovated** in 1990, everything was **photographed** before it was dismantled so that it could be put back **exactly** as it had been before.

The **ceiling** of Troubadour is adorned with stringed **instruments**. "It's the largest **collection** of American long-necked banjos outside of the British Museum I'm told." **Bruce Rogerson**, Proprietor

"I'm a **traditionalist** . . . did you know that Bach wrote thirteen harpsichord concertos to be played in the **coffee-houses** of Leipzig?" **Bruce Rogerson**, Proprietor

Troubadour was **founded** in 1955 by the Canadian, **Michael van Bloemen**. He sold the coffee-house to Bruce in 1973 and retired to Yugoslavia. However, he still **visits** London regularly.

"Bruce said he'd give me £5,000 **more** than I was asking for. I said, 'What's the **catch**?' He said 'I've got **no money**.' I said, '**Sold**.'" **Michael van Bloemen**, Former Owner

"Running this place drove me **crazy** . . . like it's driving **him** crazy." Michael van Bloemen

The downstairs room at Troubadour is a legend in its own right. Bob Dylan, Paul Simon and Jimmy Hendrix have all performed there. Current events include a regular poetry evening, a folk and blues club, classical concerts and the occasional play.

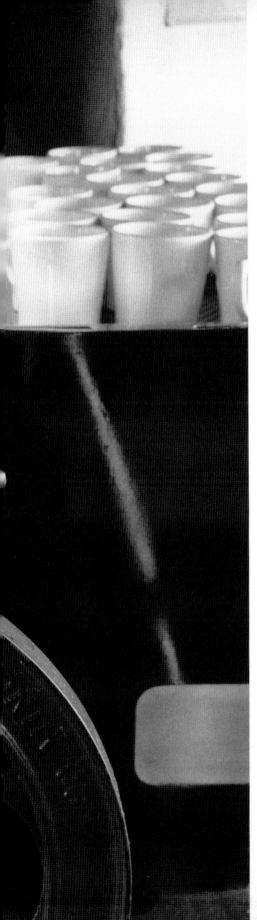

Omelette with Herbs

per serving

3 free-range eggs
dash of milk
knob of butter
1 teaspoon Herbes de Provence
pinch of fresh chopped parsley
salt and pepper to taste

Put the eggs, milk, herbs and salt and pepper into a bowl and whisk thoroughly to introduce air into the mixture. Melt the butter in a small heavy-based pan over a high heat until the butter starts frothing. Pour in the egg mixture. As it begins to cook, draw it into the centre using a spatula. Turn the heat down low and continue cooking until the mixture is solidified (if you wish to add extra ingredients such as mushrooms or bacon, these should be pre-cooked and added while the mixture is still runny in the centre). Fold the omelette over on itself in the pan, transfer to a plate and serve with salad.

179

"We like our reputation for being rude . . . but it is only if people are rude to us first."
Charlotte Bicknell, Waitress

"No one does this really . . . we all do other things. I'm a part-time student, Charlotte is an actress; it's like a family – we all keep coming back."
Isabella Meaden-Barber, Chef

Spaghetti and Rich Tomato Sauce

serves 2

1 tablespoon olive oil
1 large onion, chopped
1 medium carrot, chopped
1 stick of celery, chopped
425g (15oz) tin of plum tomatoes, sieved
1 tablespoon tomato purée
1 cup dry white wine
sea salt
fresh ground black pepper
1 teaspoon Demerara sugar
parsley stalks
2 bay leaves
½ lemon
fresh basil, coarsely chopped
2 portions of spaghetti, cooked
fresh Parmesan cheese, grated

Heat the oil in a heavy-based pan and sauté the onion, carrot and celery until soft. Add the tomatoes, tomato purée, wine, salt, pepper, sugar, parsley stalks, bay leaves and lemon. Slowly reduce over a low heat for about 1½ hours. Remove the lemon and bay leaves, sprinkle with coarsely chopped basil and serve on a bed of cooked spaghetti. Serve sprinkled with Parmesan.

WXD is a gallery as well as a café. It hosts regular exhibitions by local artists.

WXD

1 Ferme Park Road
London N4 4DS

A disused British Rail ticket office in a quiet residential area of North London may not seem like an obvious location for a café but, at the bottom of Ferme Park Road in Stroud Green, Danny Abrahamovitch, Eileen Venner and the staff of WXD have succeeded in creating a space that is all their own. Strong lines and bold colours vie for attention with an adventurous international menu, and a tranquil garden provides a perfect refuge from the rigours of London life.

WXD drinks menu...

- Coffee
  espresso. .... 80.
  double espresso. .... 1·25
  cappuccino. .... 1·00
  large cappuccino. .... 1·50
  cafe latte. .... 1·25
  mocha. .... 1·50
  (with hot milk & chocolate) ... 1·50

For some reason we are crowded on a **Wednesday**. It is the phenomenon of the mid-week date; when couples that don't live together meet up to go out midway between the weekends.

Ilse Zambonini, Manager

Danny Abrahamovitch, WXD's **effervescent** owner, borrowed the money to set up the café on his **credit card**.

I've always **loved** this building. It had been empty for about seven years, then the guy that bought it said, 'it is going to be a hairdresser's and my heart sank. I thought, 'Oh no, I can't bear another hairdresser's.'
Danny Abrahamovitch,
Proprietor

The old ticket office was formerly part of a **railway line** running from Highgate to Finsbury Park. The **tracks** have now been removed and the old cuttings and embankments have been converted into a **leafy** conservation area known as the Parkland Walk.

Danny has an oddly persuasive way with the licensing authorities. When he applied for a licence for WXD, he took plants into court and set up a garden in front of the Magistrates. "They loved it. I'm sure they are bored . . . and I gave them something to laugh at . . . but my solicitor was really embarrassed." Danny Abrahamovitch

The garden was created by Dan Pearson, winner of the Gold Award at *The Chelsea Flower Show*. The Channel Four programme, *Garden Doctors*, recorded its progress from a beer-can-strewn wilderness to a modern and imaginative herb garden.

6 We didn't want a poncy little garden with village flowers; we wanted something bold and radical. Danny Abrahamovitch 9

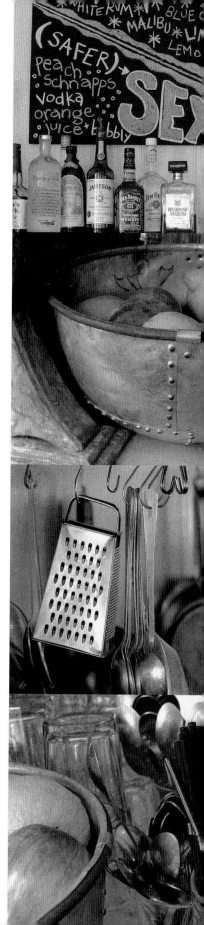

Vegetable Pakoras and Cucumber Raita   serves 2

Raita
200g (7oz) yoghurt
4cm (2in) section of cucumber, shredded
1/2 teaspoon chopped fresh mint
1/4 teaspoon cayenne pepper
salt and pepper to taste

Batter
6 heaped tablespoons of chickpea flour
1/2 teaspoon cumin seeds
1 teaspoon chopped fresh coriander
1 red chilli, finely chopped or 1/2 teaspoon cayenne pepper
1 teaspoon bicarbonate of soda
1 teaspoon turmeric
salt and fresh ground pepper to taste

Vegetables
1/2 an aubergine, thinly sliced
1 courgette, thinly sliced
4 large mushrooms, halved
2 medium onions, peeled and quartered

+ oil for deep frying

Lightly beat the yoghurt in a bowl until creamy then add the
cucumber, mint, cayenne pepper and salt and pepper to taste.
Mix the dry ingredients for the batter together in a bowl and
slowly stir in 1/2 pint of water until you have a thick batter.
Coat the vegetables thoroughly in batter and deep fry in hot oil
until golden all over. Serve with the cucumber raita.

Roasted Tomatoes with Peaches

serves 2

6 large tomatoes, halved
sea salt
fresh ground pepper
pinch of sugar
3 peaches, stoned, skinned and quartered
juice of 1/2 lemon
1 tablespoon olive oil
1/4 teaspoon cumin seeds
1 tablespoon chopped fresh coriander

Pre-heat the oven to 140C (275F/gas mark 1). Place the tomatoes face down in a baking dish and season with salt, pepper and a pinch of sugar. Slow roast in the oven on a low heat for about 4 hours or overnight. Once roasted, leave the tomatoes to cool, then mix them together with the peaches in a bowl with the lemon juice, olive oil, cumin seeds and coriander. Season to taste. Pile onto a plate and serve.

188

The fixed menu of bar **snacks** is augmented by a varied range of daily specials created by the head chef, Caroline Hamlin.

6 Last Saturday, Caroline got a spontaneous round of applause . . . what's appreciation if it doesn't involve a bit of public humiliation. 9 Danny Abrahamovitch

Amato

14 Old Compton Street W1

0171 734 5733

Open: Mon–Sat, 8am–10pm; Sun, 10am–8pm

Nearest tube: Leicester Square/Tottenham Court Road

Bar Italia

22 Frith Street W1

0171 437 4520

Open: 24 hours daily

Nearest tube: Leicester Square/Tottenham Court Road

Blue Legume

101 Stoke Newington Church Street N16

0171 923 1303

Open: Tues–Wed, 9.30am–6.30pm;

Thurs–Fri, 9.30am–11pm; Sat–10.30am–11pm;

Sun, 10.30am–6.30pm

Bus route: 73

Blue Mountain

18 North Cross Road SE22

0181 299 6953

Open: Mon–Sat, 9am–7pm; Sun, 10am–6pm

Nearest BR: East Dulwich

Bus route: 12, 40, 176, 185, 434

The Boiled Egg & Soldiers

63 Northcote Road SW11

0171 223 4894

Open: Mon–Sat, 9am–6pm; Sun, 10am–5pm

Nearest BR: Clapham Junction

Bus route: 45, 219, 319

Books for Cooks

4 Blenheim Crescent W11

0171 221 1992

Open: Mon–Sat, 9.30am–6pm

Nearest tube: Notting Hill Gate/Ladbrooke Grove

Bus route: 7, 23, 52

Candid Café

3 Torrens Street EC1

0171 278 9368

Open: daily 12 noon–10pm

Nearest Tube: Angel

The Coffee Gallery

23 Museum Street WC1

0171 436 0455

Open: Mon–Fri, 8am–5.30pm; Sat, 10am–5.30pm

Nearest tube: Holborn

Crowbar Coffee

55–57 Exmouth Market EC1

0171 833 4725

Open: Mon–Fri, 8am–8pm; Sat, 9am–5pm

Nearest tube: Farringdon

Bus route: 19, 38, 73

Cyberia

39 Whitfield Street W1

0171 209 0982

Open: Mon–Fri, 9.30am–10pm; Sat–Sun, 10am–9pm

Nearest tube: Goodge Street

The Fifth Floor Café

Harvey Nichols, Knightsbridge SW1

0171 235 5000

Open: Mon–Sat 10am–10.30pm; Sun, 12 noon–6pm

Nearest tube: Knightsbridge

Hothouse

9 Station Approach, Kew TW9

Directory

0181 332 1923
Open: daily, 10am–7pm
Nearest tube/BR: Kew Gardens

Konditor & Cook
66 The Cut, SE1
0171 620 2700
Open: Mon–Fri 8.30am–11pm; Sat, 10.30am–11pm
Nearest tube/BR: Waterloo

Maison Bertaux
28 Greek Street, W1
0171 437 6007
Open: Mon–Sat 8.30am–8pm; Sun, 9am–1pm, 3–8pm
Nearest tube: Leicester Square, Piccadilly Circus,
Tottenham Court Road

M. Manze
87 Tower Bridge Road SE1
0171 407 2985
Open: Mon, 11am–2pm; Tues–Thurs;10.30am–2pm;
Fri, 10am–2.15pm: Sat, 10am–2.45pm
Nearest tube/BR: London Bridge
Bus route: 1, 42, 188

Monmouth Coffee Company
27 Monmouth Street WC2
0171 836 5272
Open: Mon–Sat, 9am–6.30pm; Sun, 9.30am–6pm
Nearest tube: Covent Garden/Leicester Square

E. Pellicci
332 Bethnal Green Road E2
0171 739 4873
Open: Mon–Sat, 6.30am–5pm
Nearest tube/BR: Bethnal Green
Bus route: 8

The Poetry Place
22 Betterton Street WC2
0171 240 5081
Open: Tues, Thurs, Fri, 11am–11pm;
Mon, Weds, 11am–6pm; Sat, 6.30–11pm
Nearest tube: Covent Garden/Holborn

The Raj Tea Room
67 Highgate High Street N6
0181 348 8760
Open: Tues–Thurs, 9am–6pm + selected evenings;
Fri–Sat, 10am–6pm, 8–11pm
Bus route: 143, 210, 271

Tadim Café
41 Camberwell Church Street SE5
0171 708 0838
Open: daily, 8am–10pm
Bus route: 12, 36, 171

Tea Time
21 The Pavement SW4
0171 622 4944
Open: daily, 10am–6pm
Nearest tube: Clapham Common

Troubadour
265 Old Brompton Road SW5
0171 370 1434
Open: daily, 10am–11pm
Nearest tube: Earls Court/West Brompton

WXD
1 Ferme Park Road N4
0181 292 0516
Open: Mon–Fri, 12 noon–11pm; Sat–Sun, 10am–11pm
Nearest tube/BR: Finsbury Park; Bus route: W3

Index